The Coffee Fanatic's Field Guide To
Coffee, Coffee Drinks, and Coffeehouses

Matt Peach

™

Shenandoah Blue Ridge Media
Ruckersville, Virginia

Cover design and photographs by Nadia Mercer

The Coffee Fanatic's Field Guide To Coffee, Coffee Drinks, and Coffeehouses
Matt Peach

Published by:

Shenandoah Blue Ridge Media
955 Carodon Drive
Ruckersville, Virginia 22968-3187

e-mail: info@coffeefanaticsguide.com

website: http://coffeefanaticsguide.com

Copyright © 2008 by Matt Peach

All rights reserved.

No part of this book my be reproduced or transmitted in any form or manner whatsoever without permission from the author, with the exception of shorts excerpts used with acknowledgement of the publisher and author.

Library of Congress Control Number: 2007903861

ISBN: 978-0-07966091-0-7

Printed in the United States of America

Set in Palatino Linotype

First Edition

Trademarks: The Coffee Fanatic character used on the cover and throughout the book in various illustrated sizes and poses are registered trademarks of Shenandoah Blue Ridge Media and the author and may not be used without written permission. Other brands, products, etc. mentioned in this book may be the trademarks of their respective owners.

About the Author

Matt Peach started writing about coffee six years ago. Each week thousands of people enjoy Matt's commentaries explaining coffee and its history. A life long aficionado of coffee, he became a writer and author about it in a roundabout way.

Prior to 2001 he wrote resource guides and instructional manuals in addition to developing and delivering training programs for AT&T. Matt decided to combine his interest in having his own business with his life long love of coffee. In 2001 he left the corporate world and founded Shenandoah Blue Ridge Coffee, LLC, initially acquiring licenses to publish three separate editions of Coffee News® (an international franchise weekly publication) in Central Virginia. Distributing the publications through coffeehouses and restaurants, Matt soon realized that many readers desire more specific information about the subject of coffee. So, he started writing short articles about the different aspects of coffee to be included in his weekly publications.

As Matt received positive feedback from his readers who love the weekly coffee columns, he did further research about the whole subject. It was not long before he realized that there is a need for an informative guide that covers coffee, coffee drinks and coffeehouses. Drawing upon his extensive training experience coupled with his expanded knowledge of coffee, he authored this first book. He chose a field guide format as a way of explaining all the various aspects of coffee and the influence it has on our lives in a useful, yet entertaining format. He hopes you, the reader agrees!

To my wife Patricia
To my Children - Debra, Douglas, Pamela, and Sean
To my Grandchildren – Carson, MJ, & Rachel
To my son-in-law, Ed & future daughter-in-law, Sarah
-- In memory of David Peach --

Acknowledgments

I have not even considered citing all the resources and experts sourced in the writing of this book. Space would simply not be available to do so. My appreciation especially goes to:

The wonderful readers of my weekly coffee columns who were the ones that really inspired me to write this book

Many coffeehouse owners who, over the years, provided me with the equivalent of a master's degree in Coffee.

Nadia Mercer who I am particularly indebted to for designing the book cover, the Coffee Fanatic character, and for taking all the photographs used throughout the book.

Disclaimer

This book is intended as a general guide to information about the subject matter covered. It is for sale with the understanding that the author and publisher are not engaged in rendering professional services. The purpose of the book is to express the author's opinions and ideas on the topics discussed as well as to impart new information that research has uncovered. Every effort has been made to include only information that is complete and as accurate as possible. However there may be errors and mistakes in the content. Shenandoah Blue Ridge Media and the author shall have neither liability nor responsibility to any individual, company or entity for any loss or injury caused or alleged to have been caused, either directly or indirectly, by the information contained in this book.

If you do not want to be constrained by the above, you may return this book to the publisher for a full refund.

Contents

Introduction	1
Section I - What Degree Of Coffee Fanatic Are You?	3
Section II – The Field Guide	11
1 - Coffeehouse Habitats	13
2 - Identifying & Exploring Coffeehouses	29
3 - Coffee Drink Nomenclature	39
4 - Become a Coffee Barista In Your Own Home	53
5 - The Strange World Of Coffee Makers	71
6 - Putting It All Together	89

Section II – The Field Guide

7 - Exploring Other Coffee Habitats … 103

8 - The Socially Responsible, Environmentally Friendly & Politically Correct Coffee Fanatic … 113

9 - Health Taxonomy & Calories … 143

10 - The Future Of the Coffee Drinking Species … 157

Section III – The Coffee Fanatic's Recommended Resources … 167

Main Index … 181

Index to Coffee Fanatic Tips … 188

Introduction

There is a little bit of a Coffee Fanatic in all of us who love our coffee and coffee drinks. This zeal crosses all cultures, race, gender, and age groups. Those of us who drink coffee are all a little crazy about it, from the working class who can't start their morning without their "cup of Joe" to a Martha Stewart, who when asked what she missed the most while she was in prison, replied: "The only thing I've been dreaming about is a cappuccino."

Being a full-blown coffee fanatic, my fascination with all aspects of coffee and its part in our American history and culture has led to this book. Furthermore, I could not find a clear, straightforward guide for average people who love coffee and want to find out more about enjoying it. While there are certainly serious books about the coffee industry and ancient coffee history (see Section III, Recommended Resources), there is little published for the general public about our enjoyment and growing passion for all aspects of coffee, coffeehouses, and coffee drinks. *The Coffee Fanatic's Field Guide* is intended to bridge that gap, focusing on our modern coffee culture and our enthusiasm for enjoying this great drink! With no pretense of being a scholarly work, the Field Guide intends to entertain you while increasing your knowledge of this sacred brew and the various ways that we enjoy it in our society.

I am one of the millions of coffee fanatics who daily enjoy my favorite coffee drink at my local coffeehouse, in addition to brewing coffee at home. While traveling, I will go out of my way to visit a coffeehouse or other establishment in order to get a good coffee drink. I hate the aftertaste and stale flavor of many gas station coffees but you can even find me there when nothing else is available.

I used the format of a field guide to categorize all the types of information about coffee. The drink itself is fascinating but the impact upon our culture is even more intriguing. In addition, young college age Latte buyers as well as older "cup of Joe" coffee drinkers have related to me their dismay with understanding the variety or coffees, coffee drinks and coffee makers in the marketplace today. Likewise, navigating coffeehouses with their vast menus and different social structures can be very intimidating for anyone who is not a regular customer.

The Coffee Fanatic's Field Guide has been written for all you other fanatics out there who love coffee and for all you aspiring fanatics as well. I've purposely made it "light" but full of tips and other useful information. I hope reading the book will increase your enjoyment of coffee, encourage you to try different types of coffee drinks, and to visit more coffeehouses across our great land.

Section I – *What Degree of Coffee Fanatic Are You?*

The word "fanatic" associated with our book's title, "The Coffee Fanatic's Field Guide" was not chosen by happenstance. In searching for just the right word for people who love coffee and go out of their way to enjoy it, I was particularly drawn to Funk & Wagnall's Standard Dictionary Comprehensive International Edition's definition of *fanatic*: "Actuated by extravagant or intemperate zeal; inordinately and unreasonably enthusiastic." And that is exactly how we coffee drinkers are. We love our coffee and we are devoted to enhancing our overall enjoyment of coffee drinks in addition to being enthusiastic about finding and brewing a better cup of coffee at home.

Photo by Nadia Mercer

YOU ARE A COFFEE FANATIC

If you are perusing this book, I submit that you are already a Coffee Fanatic to some degree. The question is what degree of Coffee Fanatic are you?

May you start every day with a smile on your face, a song in your heart and a good cup of coffee in your hand. (An Irish saying)

Are you:

A level 1 Fanatic? – This is the basic or novice level of coffee fanaticism. You like coffee and coffee drinks – there is no turning back!

A Level 2 Fanatic? – A full-blown Coffee drinker & Lover! This is the accomplished level of coffee fanaticism.

A level 3 Fanatic? – Highly advanced level, reserved for only the most ardent coffee devotee & coffeehouse bard!

TAKE THE *COFFEE FANATIC'S* TEST

Find out where you belong on the scale of Coffee Fanatics - take our foolproof test! And don't forget the important Verification Step at the end.

Warning – *Do not try to influence the outcome of this test. These quantitative questions coupled with the test analysis methodology have been developed by a coffee fanaticism expert (the author) using a rigorous competency based model. The whole design process has been subjected to various validation and reliability studies. (Well, I did show it to a few friends who are also Coffee Fanatics.)*

Question 1. *I drink coffee:*
    A. Once a day
    B. A few Times a Day
    C. Constantly throughout the Day

Question 2. *The local coffeehouse (or the one near work):*
- A. I really don't know where it is
- B. Is a place that I visit a few times a week
- C. Is a place that I consider my second home

Question 3. *I drink coffee at home out of a:*
- A. A standard 8 Oz. coffee cup
- B. A regular size coffee mug
- C. Something resembling a large beer stein

Question 4. *When traveling*:
- A. I will get my coffee at the gas station that I stop at to fill up.
- B. I will go out of my way to find a good cup of coffee.
- C. I research good coffeehouses in advance and include them as part of my trip itinerary. (I'll even bring my own coffee in case it is not available locally.)

Question 5. *I usually have a Latte or Cappuccino:*
- A. Rarely or not at all
- B. A few times each week
- C. Most days

Question 6. *I have a coffee dependency in that*:
- A. I can't start the day without a cup.
- B. I can't start the day without a cup(s) plus I have a cup at breaks and after most meals.
- C. I can't start the day without a coffee, nor can I do anything without a cup in my hands.

Question 7. *The number of cups that I drink each day is:*
- A. 1 – 3
- B. 3 – 6
- C. 7 Plus

Question 8. *I buy my coffee at:*
- A. The local supermarket, usually selecting whatever brand is on sale.
- B. The local supermarket, selecting premium brands and making sure that they 100% Arabica beans.
- C. My local coffeehouse or coffee shop.

Question 9. *In brewing coffee at home:*
- A. I use coffee that I purchased already ground.
- B. I purchase coffee beans & custom grind it at the store.
- C. I have my own grinder (a burr type of course), and only grind the beans immediately before brewing in order to minimize the lost of flavor.

Question 10. *Each week, I spend approximately the following amount both buying coffee for home consumption and buying coffee or coffee drinks at my local coffee shop (or gas station):*
- A. $10. - $15.
- B. $15. - $25.
- C. Over $25

Question 11. *The last time I had a cup of coffee was:*
- A. Earlier today
- B. About an hour ago
- C. I'm having one right now

Question 12. *Concerning coffee and health benefits:*
- A. I am not aware of any but I love coffee so much that I don't care.
- B. I am aware of a few indirect benefits such as caffeine keeping you alert while driving.
- C. I have convinced myself that coffee is extremely beneficial to my health, is a major source of antioxidants and it reduces the risk of getting a variety of diseases.

Question 13. *For brewing coffee at home*:
- A. I recently updated my coffee brewing to an automatic Filter drip brewer with a number of features including a cone-shaped filter basket.
- B. I own a higher end automatic drip brewer model with a metal mesh cone filter and a thermos carafe to keep the coffee hot without overheating it. I am thinking of getting an espresso-brewing machine in the near future.
- C. When I take my coffee and espresso brewing equipment out, my kitchen resembles a small chemistry laboratory.

Question 14. *The average price that I pay for a cup of coffee or for a coffee drink is:*
- A. Under $1.50
- B. $1.50 - $3.
- C. Over $4.

Question 15. *I'll often have the following with coffee:*
- A. A donut or a piece of pie
- B. A biscotti, cinnamon roll, or a cookie
- C. Nothing – I believe that coffee should be enjoyed separately in order to thoroughly enjoy the aroma and flavor

Question 16. *I always educate myself about coffee by:*
- A. Reading the roaster's information that they provide on their packaging explaining their different types and blends.
- B. Questioning the coffeehouse barista or owner about their roasts and brewing equipment
- C. I own or have borrowed a book(s) about coffee from the library.

Question 17. *When ordering coffee at a restaurant:*
- A. I will frequently order a cup after my meal.
- B. Before ordering, I'll question the server about the type of coffee that they have.
- C. I'll not only inquire about the coffee type but when it was brewed (this usually motivates the server to brew a fresh pot for me).

Question 18. *The following phase most accurately reflects by feelings about coffee:*
    A. A great morning drink to wake you up and get your day going!
    B. A superb drink to be enjoyed like a fine wine!
    C. The nectar of the gods!

Substantiate the Results

This last step is needed to verify the results. While the author's insight, experience, and knowledge, influenced by caffeine-induced work sessions, has lead to this refined analysis process, we recommend you take this next step to insure the accuracy of the results.

    Verification Step – Before scoring, give the test to someone who knows you well and have them answer the questions for you. Then go back and revise your answers to more accurately reflect the true level of your coffee fanaticism.

Scoring

5 points for every **A** answer

10 Points for every **B** answer

15 Points for every **C** answer

What Level of Coffee Fanatic are you?

A score below 90 – means that you could not even answer all the questions. This is disappointing to us true Coffee Fanatics. Perhaps you have gotten this book for someone else? In any event we will not give up on you. Read on!

90-140 – You are a bona fide Coffee Fanatic, albeit a novice at **Level 1**. But we want to encourage you to apply yourself even further & we stand ready to support your growing commitment.

145-225 – As a full-blown **Level 2 Coffee Fanatic**, you should be quite proud of this achievement. We are duly impressed.

230-270 - Speaking on behalf of all advanced Coffee Fanatics, Congratulations! As a **Level 3 Coffee Fanatic**, you are our type of people!

No coffee can be good in the mouth that does not first send a sweet offering of odor to the nostrils.

(Henry Ward Beecher)

Section II *The Field Guide*

Chapter 1 – Coffeehouse Habitats

Chapter 2 – Identifying & Exploring Coffeehouses

Chapter 3 – Coffee Drink Nomenclature

Chapter 4 – Become a Coffee Barista In Your Own Home

Chapter 5 – The Strange World Of Coffee Makers

Chapter 6 – Putting It All Together

Chapter 7 – Exploring Other Coffee Habitats

Chapter 8 – The Socially Responsible, Environmentally Friendly and Politically Correct Coffee Fanatic

Chapter 9 – Health Taxonomy & Calories

Chapter 10 – The Future of the Coffee Drinking Species ™

Ah! How sweet coffee tastes. Lovelier than a thousand kisses, sweeter far than muscatel wine!

("Coffee Cantata" - J.S. Bach)

Chapter 1 – Coffeehouse Habitats

Field Guide Chapter 1 Highlights
- *Coffeehouse habitats*
- *World-wide habitat history*
- *Today's coffeehouse habitats*
  (Blame it on the Italians & Starbucks)
- *The emergence of an American coffee culture*

Any worthy field guide addresses the habitat of the species that it is covering in considerable detail. This Field Guide is no exception, for aside from those Coffee Fanatics that just drink their coffee at home, the place that you will find most Coffee Fanatics is at the coffeehouses and coffee shops of our land. The purpose of this chapter and succeeding chapters is to help aspiring and experienced Coffee Fanatics alike to understand and navigate our modern coffeehouse habitats. Coffeehouses are magnificent in their simplicity yet they are increasingly complex in the varieties of their offerings and in their social culture, which certainly is exhibited by the cross section of people who frequent them.

Every advanced *Coffee Fanatic* knows that you do not haphazardly walk into a coffee shop and ask for a "cup of Joe," pay for it and immediately leave. (People on their way to work are, of course, the exception.) Coffeehouse habitats are just that, a habitat and many Coffee Fanatics spend a lot of time in them on a daily basis. These environments should be enjoyed for the overall experience that they offer. If your favorite one is carefully selected, it will offer you a refuge from the stresses of everyday life. In addition, all levels of

Coffee Fanatics need to know about and enjoy the various coffee selections and other amenities that coffeehouses offer to the fullest. After all, you would not go into a fine bakery and ask for a plain donut, enter a better wine shop and just request a jug wine, or ask a cheese shop if it has Velveeta.

Habitat Evolution

America's modern coffeehouses truly represent a unique evolution of an ancient concept. The number and popularity of our coffeehouses was accomplished through amazing American creativity, entrepreneurship and marketing ingenuity. While the rest of the world is cringing thinking about what we have done to coffee and especially espresso-brewed coffee drinks, we Americans have come to enjoy a wide variety of these drinks, both hot and cold. Our love of coffee has afforded countless opportunities for entrepreneurs, baristas, and other employees of coffeehouses, roasting facilities, and in the overall coffee and coffee specialty industry.

A global perspective is needed as well as a national one to appreciate coffeehouses and the impact they are making on our culture and to gain an understanding of how today's coffeehouses have evolved.

Coffeehouses Around the World

As early as the 15th Century, you could get a cup of coffee (but regrettably, some might say, not a Latte) at the world's first coffeehouse in Mecca, established in 1475. People gathered there to meet friends, exchange ideas and discuss the issues of the day, read and to enjoy music, art or poetry. (Not much has changed in that regard today except for the addition of the PC and access to the Internet)

As coffee began to be enjoyed as a drink rather than for medicinal purposes (which was the case from about 525 AD through the 1400's.), Coffeehouses sprang up throughout Europe, first enjoyed by the aristocrats who imported it from the ports of Mocha in Yemen or Java, off of Indonesia. (Named after theses seaport cities, Mocha and Java were also the names of some of the most popular coffees of the day and not some brainchild of a coffee drink marketing executive.) England got its first coffeehouse in 1650, Paris in 1672, Venice in 1700, and Berlin in 1721. At the start of the 18th Century, there were already approximately 2,000 coffeehouses in London. In their early history, coffeehouses have been both banned or closed down by various governmental regimes. This was because the rulers became suspicious of the evolutionary or anti- government planning that was being carried out in them. See Section III for a list of books that cover this early history in extensive detail.

American Coffeehouses
(Was that George Washington ordering a Grande latte?)

Coffeehouses were in America since the late Seventeenth Century in cities such as Boston, New York, and Philadelphia. In one of the most famous ones, The Green Dragon in Boston (existed between 1697 and 1832), you could find the likes of Paul Revere and John Adams commiserating about the British rule of the Colonies. In fact, the Green Dragon was called by some, "The Headquarters of the American Revolution." New York City had The Tontine coffeehouse where the New York Stock Exchange got its start and over in Philadelphia, you could on rare occasion, meet George Washington or Thomas Jefferson at the Merchants Coffee House. The city of New Orleans whose coffeehouse culture started under French rule in the eighteen century, boasted many coffeehouses (called Exchanges) before it became part of America through the Louisiana Purchase in 1803.

In the early days of America's thirst for coffee, you could probably always count on a better cup at a coffeehouse than you could make at home (not much has changed today especially if you like espresso). Most Americans around 1850 for example roasted coffee beans that they purchased in a frying pan, ground them and then boiled the coffee grinds in water. They used various means to separate the brewed coffee from the grinds. Many of the coffeehouses not only had professional roasting equipment but also utilized better brewing methods to make their coffee.

Today's Coffeehouse Habitat
Blame It on the Italians & Starbucks

Influence of the Espresso Machine The abundance and popularity of today's coffeehouses, not only in America but also around the world, were originally due to the invention of the Espresso Machine. Simply put, the average citizen cannot duplicate the quality of espresso (the main ingredient for most coffee drinks) served in Coffeehouses. This is because they have the best equipment and it is expensive. Most people do not have or want to spend over $1,000 of their disposable income on a first class espresso machine. In ancient history, coffeehouses were the only places where people could buy coffee. The espresso machine, first invented in 1821, perfected the art of brewing a strongly roasted coffee that was so enjoyed by Italians and other Southern Europeans. In espresso brewing water is heated and pressure-forced through finely ground coffee in about 20 seconds. The process maximizes the flavor and aroma of the drink. The early machines were huge and specifically made for coffeehouses and restaurants. Kenneth

Davids in his book, "*Coffee*" said it best, "*The espresso brewing machine is the spiritual heart and aesthetic centerpiece of the great coffee places, the cafés, caffés, and coffeehouses of the world.*"

Modern Espresso brewing equipment - Photo by Nadia Mercer

Purchasing this type of coffee making equipment, except for some of the most ardent Coffee Fanatics, is low on the priority list of household appliances to own, after refrigerators, washers, dryers, etc. Moreover, even as we become more able to duplicate espresso-based coffee drinks at home economically, going to a coffeehouse is akin to "going out to the movies" in our modern society when we can conveniently download or rent almost any movie that we want. For a number of reasons, the experience of going to a coffeehouse is becoming forever ingrained in American culture.

Starbucks' Influence Along with the espresso machine, Starbucks changed the culture of coffeehouses and coffee drinks in America dramatically starting in the 1980's.

Founded in Seattle in 1971, Starbucks started their expansion of stores in 1983 after their marketing director visited Italy and saw first hand the proliferation of coffeehouses and their culture. Equally important, they started to experiment with the various types and sizes of espresso-based drinks that are sold today in Starbucks. The lattes (heretofore a breakfast drink only in Europe) and cappuccino variations offered, not to mention the congenial habitat that Starbucks created in each and every coffeehouse, brought a whole new younger generation of coffee drinkers plus many business people into coffeehouses for the first time.

Both Starbucks as well as other coffeehouse chains in addition to the many independent coffeehouses in America have flourished ever since.

A Distinctly American Coffee Habitat & Culture Emerges

As early as the 1860's, Arbuckle Brothers, a wholesale grocer in Pittsburgh started marketing and selling roasted coffee beans under the "Ariosa" brand name. This started a boom in coffee sales across America and, by the end of the nineteenth century; other companies had started into the coffee roasting business including Chase & Sanborn, Folgers, Maxwell House, and the A & P Company. Because of Arbuckle Brothers and other American roasting companies, the dawn of the twentieth century found most Americans no longer using frying pans to roast their coffee beans. There was also a marked improvement in the taste of the coffee purchased from professionals in the roasting business.

During this period, coffeehouses in America continued to prosper because they offered far more than a "cup of Joe." They were primarily a place to go to exchange ideas, to discuss the leading issues of the day, to read, to relax, and to enjoy an extremely creative atmosphere.

The consumption of coffee and growth of coffeehouses continued to mushroom throughout the 20th. Century along with the growth of America. The quality of coffee varied greatly from the late 1800's, when coffee beans and ground coffee (as opposed to green coffee beans that had to be roasted) was first sold to the general public, through approximately the mid-1900's since there was little regulation or truth in-advertising laws. Inferior and stale coffee was frequently sold as well as coffee that was diluted with various substances. One of the common items was chicory roots, which is preferred by many French people in their coffee and is very popular today in New Orleans. There was a long and diverse list of other additives employed by unscrupulous business people including chickpeas, holly berries, figs, barley, carob beans, and sunflower seeds.

Key Dates Influencing American Coffee Culture

Some significant events surrounding the development of a distinctive American coffee culture, our coffee consumption and coffeehouse habitats are as follows:

1800's – As Americans started settling the western part of the United States, green coffee beans were always high on their supply list of things to take on the long wagon ride. In fact, many of these beans were often traded to Native American Indians, who also started to enjoy this enchanting drink. By the latter part of the century, the term "Cowboy Coffee" became part of our coffee lexicon. It was used to refer to the way cowboys roasted their beans in a frying pan over a fire while out on the range.

1833 – The first commercial coffee roaster was brought into the United States from London, England.

1850 – The Folgers Coffee Company (now owned by Proctor & Gamble) was officially started when Jim Folger started a coffee roasting company in San Francisco perceptively forecasting a market for coffee due to all the new people that were migrating West during America's great Gold Rush.

1859 – The Great Atlantic and Pacific Tea Company (A & P) was started. Within 10 years, they were selling coffee directly to consumers through over 5000 horse drawn wagons. By 1915, they were selling coffee through a network of over 7000 stores.

1860's – It became possible to package roasted coffee beans and store them for a reasonable length of time (and ship them to other cities) through the development of a stronger and more resilient coffee bag. This packaging material along with the commercial coffee roaster gave birth to the development of the coffee roasting business across America.

1864 – Arbuckles became the first company to package and sell roasted coffee beans. They established huge roasting plants in Chicago, Kansas City and New York and packaged their beans in 1Lb. bags. By the turn of the Century, they even owned a shipping fleet and had an office in South America.

1878 – Chase & Sanborn became the first company to put coffee in sealed tins.

By 1900 – Manual coffee grinders started to be used for the first time in middle to upper class households across America.

1900 – Hills Brothers developed a way to preserve the freshness of roasted coffee beans longer by packaging them in vacuum-sealed tins. They were able sell their coffee to a greater number of states because of this new process.

Early 1900's - The city of New Orleans had the most coffeehouses (a few hundred of them known as "exchanges") in America because of their long history of being the primary port for coffee imports from South America.

1901-1902 – Barcalo Manufacturing company in Buffalo, New York started giving its employees coffee breaks for the first time, even though they did not use the exact term. (The official words, "Coffee Break" were introduced by the Pan-American Coffee Bureau in advertisements used in 1952.)

1901 - 1910 – The demand for better quality and quantity increased as, a major wave of new coffee-drinking immigrants (approximately 9 million) came to United States from Europe. This added to the European immigrant population that had started to migrate to America as early as 1840.

1907 –President Teddy Roosevelt coined the first major advertising slogan for coffee when he was served Maxwell coffee at the Hermitage Hotel in Nashville, Tennessee. He said the coffee was "***good to the last drop***" and that became an advertising slogan for Maxwell House for over 50 years.

1916 - The M.E. Swing Company was started in Washington, D.C. The company specialized in selling better-roasted coffee beans. Ultimately, they started selling brewed coffee in their store turning it into a quasi-coffeehouse.

1920's – Coffeehouse opened in major cities across America and coffee beans sales reached new highs because of Prohibition in America

1921-1928 – Alice MacDougall became the first woman to open a chain of coffeehouses (5) in New York City

1927 – Reggio's opened as an Italian coffeehouse in New York City. They imported and installed the first espresso machine in America. This large and magnificent La Pavoni machine can still be seen there today.

1933 – Chock-full o' Nuts owner William Black, recognizing America's growing love affair with coffee, transformed his eighteen nut shops into coffee shops in New York City.

1938 – The first reasonably good tasting instant coffee was developed by the Swiss owned Nescafé Company. (Today they own Chase & Sanborn, Hills Brothers, Taster's Choice, Sarks, MJB, and the Nescafé brands)

Pre World War II – Most Americans brewed their coffee in a stovetop percolator from the early 1900's through approximately 1945. Few knew at the time that the percolation process itself (which required constant boiling water to be drawn up through the center of the coffee pot) resulted in an over extracted and bitter tasting drink. However, for people born and brought up during that era, who can ever forget that great smell of coffee that saturated the whole house whenever coffee was brewing?

By the time the war started, America had become the number one consumer of coffee, importing over 70% of the world's coffee production. In addition, the A& P Company was the largest buyer of coffee on the World markets.

Note: A & P sold coffee fresh through three different brands: *Red Circle*, *Bokar* (a premium roast) and *Eight O'Clock*. The consumer could grind it to their liking right at the time of purchase in the store. A feature, of course, that exists in most supermarkets today. (*Eight O'Clock Coffee* still exists today and is an excellent 100% Arabica Bean coffee sold in a variety of roasts and at a reasonable price in many different supermarkets across America.)

Chapter 1 Coffeehouse Habitats - 23

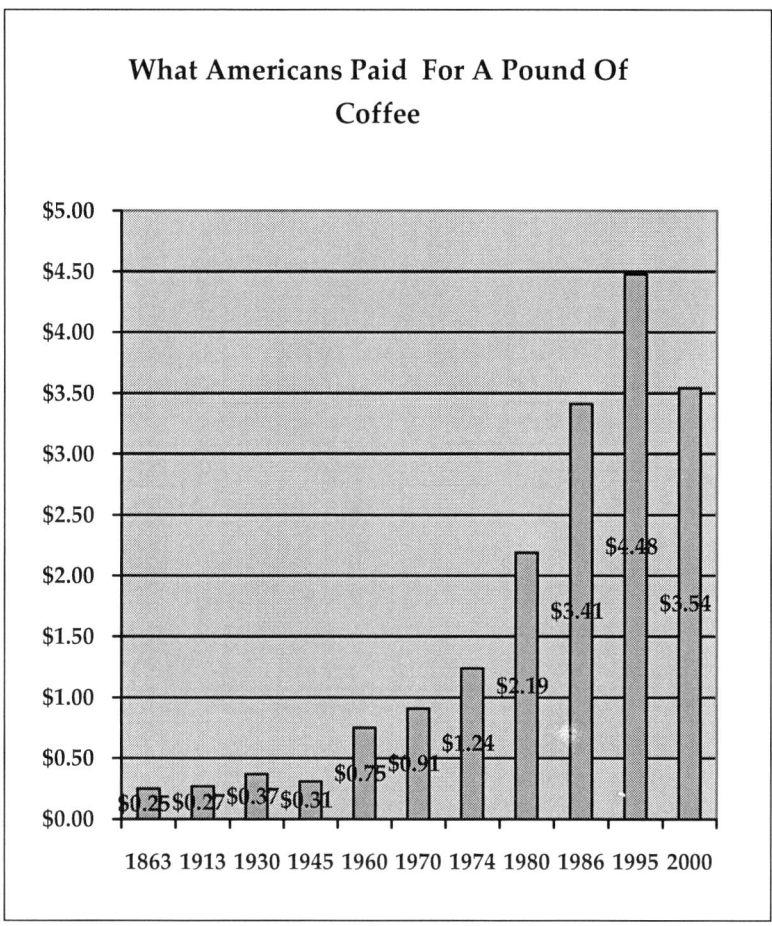

Prices mostly from *"The Value of a Dollar"* by Scott Derks, Third Edition, 2004, Grey House Publishing, Inc.

Post World War II - 1950's - Numerous dinners, luncheonettes, and small cafes are started across America, serving among other things, a good cup of coffee. Many people were known to both frequent and switch dinners based on the quality of the coffee served.

American soldiers had been given vast supplies of coffee (both regular & instant) during the war. They were not rationed like the average citizens who received coffee stamps enabling them to purchase only 1 Lb. every 5 weeks. As a result, the soldiers, known as GI Joes, drink coffee constantly. By the end of the War, the expression, "*Cuppa Joe*" became ingrained in American coffee culture.

1947 – The first coffee vending machine was invented. It dispensed hot instant coffee and by the mid-1950's, there was over 65 thousand of them across America.

1952 – The Pan-American Coffee Bureau coins the term, *coffee break* and it almost immediately becomes part of America's lexicon, and a "bargained-for" benefit in numerous management-labor contracts of our largest corporations.

1953 - Chock full o' Nuts became the first coffeehouse chain to introduce its own brand of coffee beans.

1956 – The coffeehouse, Caffè Trieste opened in the North Beach section of San Francisco, owned by Giannio Giotta. The Trieste becomes a gathering place for the "Beat" and "Hippie" generation.

1960's – Independent coffeehouses, especially on the East and West coasts became gathering places for the anti-Vietnam War protests, civil rights movement, and counter-culture activists. Many of these coffeehouses are still in business today.

1964 – General Foods came out with the first freeze-dried coffee call Maxium.

1960 – The National Federation of Columbian Coffee Growers came out with a major advertising campaign in America to encourage the sale of Columbian coffee. They created the character, *Juan Valdez* to emphasize the quality of Columbian coffee. This campaign was a major success and had a "push-pull" marketing effect that caused many coffee companies and restaurants in America to switch to

Columbian coffee because of requests from their customers. Even today, some American consumers will insist that they want only 100% Columbian coffee.

1966 – Two key events took place on opposite coasts that most likely marked the beginning of the Gourmet or Specialty coffee business in the United States. Alfred Peet started "Peets Coffee & Tea" in Berkeley, California. He began selecting better quality coffee beans from various countries and roasting those beans using methods learned while in his family's business in Holland. Alfred Peet became known as "the grandfather of specialty coffee." In the same year, Zabars, a New York City Produce store started selling world class Arabica coffee beans from the finest coffee growing regions of the world.

1970's – Mr. Coffee developed the first mass-marketed automatic drip coffee pot replacing the peculator method for most Americans. It was advertised extensibility on television by an American baseball hero, Joe DiMaggio.

1971 – Gordon Bowker, Jerry Baldwin, and Zev Siegl, trained by Alfred Peet, started Starbucks at Seattle, Washington's Pike Place Market.

1979 – Eight O'Clock Coffee became one of the first major coffee roasters to switch from using a blend of coffee beans to 100% Arabica beans. Frequently the blends of major coffee companies at that time consisted of a percentage of Robusta coffee as well as coffee from different countries.

1980 – A Swiss Water Process was developed for decaffeinating coffee. This process offered a better tasting coffee compared to the chemical method used to remove caffeine

1985 – By the mid-1980's, coffee roasters started using the Italian invention of a freshness valve that are on most coffee bags sold today. This one-way device allows carbon dioxide to escape from the bag but does not let oxygen in. Using bags with these valves preserves the freshness of coffee beans for up to nine months.

1983 – Starbucks hired Howard Schultz as director of retail operations and marketing. Upon returning from a trip to Italy in 1984, where he was impressed with their many espresso shops and bars, he convinced the founders to try this European coffeehouse approach. As a result, the first Starbucks caffè latte was served, a basic store design model was created and the expansion of this major company was started across America. Ultimately, Starbucks expanded, and is still expanding, across America and to other countries around the world.

1995 – Proctor and Gamble purchased the regional Millstone Coffee Company and expanded it nationally, selling a variety of gourmet coffee beans and special roasts through supermarkets. Interestingly, the company had originally grown into regional prominence when a much smaller Millstone acquired the supermarket distribution division, Blue Anchor from Starbucks in the mid 1980's.

1990's to Present - Coffee companies and coffeehouse franchises, as well as independent owners established shops and coffee bars across America. Today's clientele while still including the types of people that frequented coffeehouses in the 1960's, now also consist of younger people and the middle to upper class members of society. In addition to traditional coffeehouse settings, you can find your favorite latte or cappuccino in bookstores, malls, supermarkets, and even upscale gas stations. There are over 20,000 such establishments in America today.

2007 – America is the world's largest buyer of coffee, importing 2 ½ to 3 million pounds annually. Over 50% of the population drinks coffee every day. (Starbucks exceeds 10,000 locations worldwide.)

Chapter 1 Coffeehouse Habitats - 27

Reflections of Coffeehouse Culture – a Photo by Nadia Mercer Walker Tufts (left), an artist and Bryan Whitten (right), a James Madison University student sip coffee at a local coffeehouse in Harrisonburg, Virginia

Coffee information from around the world

Africa Raw coffee beans are soaked in water & spices and chewed like candy in many parts of Africa.

Australia By 1896, coffee plants had made there way to Queensland, Australia.

Brazil Coffee plants were brought to Brazil by France. They where first cultivated in1727. Now Brazil harvests approximately 1/3 of the world's production.

Costa Rica Coffee is mainly attributed to transforming Costa Rica from a backward country into a relatively modern republic with a 90% literacy rate. In 1830, the government, recognizing the potential of coffee, required every family to grow coffee trees on their land.

England Lloyd's of London began as Edward Lloyd's Coffeehouse.

Greece and Turkey The oldest person is most always served their coffee first in these two countries.

Haiti The Jesuits started growing coffee in Haiti about 1715.

Italy In Italy espresso is considered essential to daily life. The price is regulated by the government. Drinking espresso in Italy is a separate event from the main meal. There are over 200,000 coffee bars in Italy.

Japan now ranks number 3 in the world for coffee consumption. In Tokyo alone, there are over 10,000 coffee cafes plus several thousand coffee vending machines.

Martinique France brought coffee trees to Martinique in 1720.

Chapter 2 – Identifying & Exploring Coffeehouses

Field Guide Chapter 2 Highlights
- *Coffeehouse culture*
- *Identifying your breed of coffeehouse*
- *How do you know when you have discovered a good one?*

Description and Culture

While Chapter 1 furnished background on Coffeehouse habitats from the past to the present, this chapter focuses on descriptions of good coffeehouses and how to discover one that matches your personality and interests. Coffeehouses in some American cities can be found on almost every block. With approximately 20,000 coffee shops of various sizes and shapes in America, there are many theories explaining why they are so popular today. Has our society become so fast paced that the comfortable, friendly coffeehouse is a welcomed safe haven to many people? While the quality of the coffee and coffee drinks are certainly important, many people have agreed, "It's not just the coffee" that attracts us to coffeehouses.

Once you find your ideal coffeehouse, it is like embarking upon a lasting marriage; you bond forever. (Author Unknown)

So, What Does A Coffeehouse Represent For You?

The Patio of the Daily Grind Coffeehouse, Harrisonburg, VA
Photo by Nadia Mercer

an escape from daily life?
a place to study?
a place to plan?
a place for tutoring?
a place to read?
a place to listen to music?
a place to listen to poetry?
a place to relax?
a place to create – perhaps a book or a play?
a place to reflect and think?
a place to work?
a place to access the internet?
a place to interview for work?
a place to negotiate a business deal?
a place to meet people?
a place to "people-watch"?
a place to eavesdrop on?
a place to engage in meaningful conversation?

We Coffee Fanatics go to coffeehouses for all of the aforementioned reasons and probably a number of other ones as well. Plus even the most novice coffee lover knows that you can always count on getting a fresh an excellent cup of coffee or coffee drink at a coffeehouse. Many of us upon entering a coffeehouse almost immediately shed the worries and stresses of our everyday life and work. What better surroundings are there to enjoy our favorite coffee, hang out for as long as we would like and do whatever else we care to (and for a small price)?

Avg. Coffee Shop Prices in the Past (For their Coffee of the Day)	
Year	$
1700	1 Penny*
1940	.05
1950	.10
1954	.20
1975	.65
1985	.75
2000	$1.40
2007	$1.85
*In 1700 England, coffeehouses were known as Penny Universities because of what they charged. (All other prices are American.)	

Coffeehouses in America, as pointed out in Chapter 1, have morphed from early Middle Eastern and European versions into becoming truly American institutions, ingrained into our culture – as American as baseball and apple pie. If you love coffee and you don't frequent coffeehouses, you certainly have to start! Great coffee, professionals to roast it (sometimes on site) and make it, and the ambiance of

American coffeehouse culture – as the French say, "On ne peut désirer ce qu'on ne connaît pas."(You cannot desire what you do not know. - Voltaire)

Identifying A Coffeehouse For Your Use

Because of the many uses of coffeehouses, it is difficult to describe a typical one. They are all so different and diverse in their appeal. Even the individual shops of the major chains are different depending upon a number of factors. Most people who frequent coffeehouses agree that it is not the structure, décor, or name that defines the coffeehouse, but it is the people. This starts with the owner or manager who more than anyone else establishes the atmosphere and culture of the coffeehouse. The people that the owner hires, as well as the people who frequent the coffeehouse all contribute to the overall mood or atmosphere of a coffeehouse.

Many owners do plan their location and marketing to attract a particular clientele. The coffeehouses located near colleges are a prime example of this. Other college coffeehouses, whether by design or accident, attract business people during the day and students in the evening.

Some owners have even designed their coffeehouses to appeal to parents with toddlers, including a small play area. In addition to traditional, stand-alone coffeehouses, some other Coffeehouse types usually by design are:

Coffeehouses within a book store

Coffeehouses within an Art Gallery

Coffeehouses within a music store

Coffeehouses that are part of a theater

Coffeehouses that also roast and sell their own coffee

Coffeehouses that are primarily a Bakery

Coffeehouses that are primarily a Deli

Shopping Mall Coffee Bars

Coffeehouses within an office building

Coffee bars within modern gas stations

The franchises of course create coffeehouses very well as they have it down to a science. They study where the coffeehouse should be located, the clientele that they want to attract, and then they modify their successful model to fit the local circumstances. They of course also pay a great deal of attention to hiring and training their people. While you will always know what you are getting with a franchise coffeehouse (a comforting thought when it comes to coffee drink quality and also when in a strange city), you will be missing out on some great coffeehouse experiences if you don't try some of the independents. Many of them are indeed unique and are an important part of the culture of many neighborhoods across America. They also make great coffee and coffee drinks.

With both the franchises and the independents, you will find geographical differences among coffeehouses in terms of their customers. In some Northeastern cities, for example, you will find a high percentage of coffeehouses that cater to grad students, professors, and the upper middle class. In the certain West Coast cities, the coffeehouse culture more represents the high-tech, Silicone Valley culture that permeates the lifestyle there. An exception being in the Hollywood area which caters to artistic types like writers and actors associated with the movie and entertainment industry.

Mural on entrance wall of Artful
Dodger coffeehouse - see profile on next page
Photo by Nadia Mercer

\multicolumn{2}{c	}{**PROFILE OF AN INDEPENDENTLY OWNED COFFEEHOUSE**}
Name	*Artful Dodger Coffeehouse & Lounge*
Location	47 Court Square, Harrisonburg, Virginia
Established	For 15 years
Owners	Chris Clark, Ken Keck, Warren Picciolo
Clientele	Diverse – James Madison University students, Courthouse staff, lawyers, police, business people, etc.
Decor	Eclectic – including murals, art, sculpture, & Art Deco furniture
Atmosphere	Friendly & warm – the students, especially, love the place
Seating	Vast array - from outdoor to indoor – sofas, chairs, tables, stools, a long sit-down counter, plus stand-up counters.
Coffees	Specialty coffees from the prime coffee growing regions of the world
Coffee Drinks	Full range of espresso-based drinks plus a variety of cold drinks
Food	Breakfast, lunch & in-between – from pastries to wraps & sandwiches
Entertainment	Live performances on certain evenings, open poetry readings, etc.
Internet	Yes, they became a wired cybercafé in 2001 & now offer Wireless Internet
Reading Material	A wide variety including books, newspapers, newsletters, & flyers

Different Varieties of the Same Species

Some people prefer the crisp, yet cozy atmosphere of a "chain" like Daily Grind Coffee House and Café (above).

While others like the informal, eclectic type of an independent coffeehouse like the Artful Dodger.

(Both photos by Nadia Mercer)

In Search Of a Rare Breed

How does a true Coffee Fanatic go about recognizing or finding a coffeehouse that they can be happy with? As you probably have already surmised and we hope this chapter has motivated you in that direction, I strongly recommend that you visit many coffeehouses, both franchise and independents alike, take in the atmosphere and sample their drinks. Then select one or two that meet your needs and that you are comfortable in. Above all, keep an open mind; perhaps visit a coffeehouse a few times so that you can evaluate it properly.

If you travel a lot, here is a list of some of the popular franchise chains and their websites:

Caribou Coffee - www.cariboucoffee.com
Daily Grind - www.dailygrindunwind.com
Gloria Jeans - www.gloriajeans.com
Port City Java - www.portcityjava.com
Seattle's Best – www.seattlesbest.com
Starbucks - www.starbucks.com
The Coffee Bean - www.coffeebean.com
The Coffee Beanery - www.coffeebeanery.com
Tullys - www.spinelli-coffee.com

Also when hunting for a coffeehouse, keep a sense of humor. For example, evaluate your prospective coffeehouse against the Coffee Fanatic's measuring criteria? (See "You Have Found a Good Coffeehouse When:" on next page.)

You Have Found A Good Coffeehouse When:

- You can't see through the windows because there are so many flyers and announcements taped to them.

- The People inside look weirder than you do.

- The owner looks the weirdest of all.

- You order "a COD with a Depth Charge. " No one looks at you like your from out of space but they actually give you the Coffee Of the Day with a shot of espresso".

- The music sounds a lot different from the piped-in music at work or in your office building elevator.

- The art on the walls also looks different. Perhaps it is because you have not seen this art before in 10,000 other places.

- The chairs are as comfortable as the one at home that you refuse to get rid of.

- You nurse a cappuccino for 3 hours and no one asks you to leave.

- You don't understand half the conversations that you eavesdrop on.

- After meeting some of the regulars, you realize that your liberal views are really quite conservative in comparison.

- It just smells good - like coffee!

Chapter 3 – Coffee Drink Nomenclature

(Order Like A True Barista)

Nadia Mercer, Cover Designer and part time Barista at Shanks Bakery & Coffee Shop in Harrisonburg, Virginia

Field Guide Chapter 3 Highlights

- *Understanding different coffee drinks*
- *Interpreting the language of the natives*
- *Ordering your drink correctly*

This chapter is especially for you: If coffeehouse menus ranging from simple espressos to a mocha café lattes have overwhelmed you. If you shy away from coffeehouses because you don't feel comfortable ordering. If you would like to try other drinks but only know how to order a cappuccino. Or if you simply want to impress your friends by actually talking like a true coffeehouse barista.

Nowadays the coffeehouse scene can be quite demoralizing to most of us. It's not just the very knowledgeable order takers and baristas, but the people in line with you (all experienced pros, you assume) who together can represent a very intermediating culture for the up and coming Coffee Fanatic. You may be a tenured professor at the local university, working on your PhD, or attending school on a full scholarship but it is all meaningless if you can't navigate the coffeehouses and order a customized drink for your self without sounding stupid. Thank heavens for this *Coffee Fanatic's Field Guide!* We are here to help with three easy steps to enable you to order like a true barista.

Step 1. Understanding different coffee drinks

Step 2. Interpreting the language of the natives

Step 3. Ordering your drink correctly

Coffeehouses around the country, whether they are franchises or independently owned, carry the same basic drinks. Oh, they occasionally have some variations of the basic drinks. Once you know the basic drinks however, you will be easily able to question the barista about their "Lattemochaccino" or whatever the local drink is called, to see if you want to try it. Local coffeehouse owners do experiment and develop some excellent drinks – like the joy of visiting different vineyards; many coffee fanatics get pleasure from the exploration and discovery of different drinks.

As pointed out in Chapter 1, *Coffeehouse Habitats*, espresso-brewed coffee is the main ingredient in most of the drinks and a big reason why coffeehouses are so popular. They have the proper equipment and knowledge to make espresso so much better than you can at home. Like the town's best steak house that buys cuts and grades of beef that the average consumer can't, coffeehouses also have access to the best and freshest roasts and blends of coffee beans. Indeed, some establishments even roast their coffee right on the premises. When you understand one coffeehouse's menu of espresso drink offerings (and even some of the non-espresso-based drinks), you will have no trouble walking into any café in America and understanding their selections. This goes for franchise locations and independents, alike. Let's start with a universal menu of coffee drinks that you will probably find in most American coffeehouses (see next page).

Understanding these nine drinks offers the key to understanding any coffeehouse's offerings and the numerous ways that you can modify and customized your drink. (And believe it, there are countless possibilities and variations, as only we Americans would have it.)

The variety of cup sizes that you might see at a typical coffeehouse.
Photo by Nadia Mercer

Step 1. Understanding different coffee drinks

TYPICAL COFFEEHOUSE MENU

Espresso

Espresso Macchiato

Espresso con Panna

Americano

Cappuccino

Latte

Mocha

Café Au Lait

Coffee of the Day

Photo by Nadia Mercer

Espresso – The heart of most coffee drinks, espresso is a made in a special brewing machine from dark roasted beans. The coffee is finely ground just before brewing. The espresso brewing machine forces heated water (about 195° F.) through the coffee in less than 25 seconds preserving the strong aroma and flavor of the coffee. Historically served in a one shot measurement of 1½ Ozs., people who drink it straight, usually add sugar, and are served the shot in a demitasse cup (as you see in this picture) by the more traditional coffeehouses. Some espresso drinkers will rub a lemon peel on the top of the cup to enhance the taste (called an *Espresso Romano).*

Espresso Macchiato – a shot of espresso serve in a demitasse or other small cup that has a small amount of frothed milk on the top.

Espresso con Panna – A shot of espresso served with a dollop of whipped cream on the top.

Americano – Named after us wimpy Americans who want to dilute everything including the basic espresso. It consists of a shot of espresso mixed with about 1 cup of hot water and normally served in a small cup. Some people will order a double shot of espresso (called a *Doppio)* and change the water content accordingly.

Cappuccino – There are many disputes on how to make an authentic cappuccino especially when you talk to Italian Americans. The American cappuccino served in most coffeehouses today consists of 1/3 Espresso, 1/3 steamed milk, and 1/3 frothed milk. It is also frequently garnished with cocoa, cinnamon, or nutmeg.

Latte – The American coffeehouse latte consists of approximately ¼ espresso and ¾ steamed milk, with about a ¼ inch of frothed milk added on top. It is not an exact science and the proportions vary from coffeehouse to coffeehouse. Surface it to say that, unlike a cappuccino, there is plenty of milk compared to the amount of espresso. It may even be 1/5 espresso to 4/5 milk ratios in some establishments. Also the mixture will vary by the number of shots you order and the size of the drink cup. Baristas will adjust the volume of milk to fit the size of the drink. To make sure that you a getting a balanced latte, you should generally order a regular latte (with a single shot of espresso) for a Small drink (8 Oz. Cup), a double shot for a Tall (12 Oz. Cup), a triple for a Grande (16 Oz. Cup), and a quad (4 shots with a Venti (20 Oz. Cup).

Lattes are the most popular coffeehouse drinks and they come in many variations. Most coffeehouses offer 6 to 10 different flavors that mix well with coffee such as a *Hazelnut Latte* or a *Vanilla Latte*. In addition you can add sugar, whip cream, and different garnishes.

Mocha – *Mochas* are usually listed on coffeehouse menus either as *Mocha Lattes*, *Moccaccinos*, or just plain *Mochas*. Mocha of course implies the addition of chocolate, usually chocolate syrup to either a latte or a cappuccino. It pays to inquire about the ingredients and mix of espresso and milk to determine whether you are really ordering a chocolate cappuccino or a chocolate latte. A few traditional coffeehouses still serve the original Mocha drink that originated about 50 years ago which consists of 1/3 espresso, 1/3 steamed milk and 1/3 hot chocolate, with whip cream on top.

Café Au Lait – There is no espresso in this drink. It consists of ½ regular brewed coffee and ½ hot milk.

Coffee of the Day – This is where the local coffeehouse will list their featured brewed coffee that day. Some people do not realize that in addition to espresso-based drinks. You can get some outstanding regular coffee from all over the world at your local coffeehouse. In addition to their featured Coffee of the Day, most coffeehouses will carry regular coffee in different roasts from mild to extremely strong in addition to decaffeinated coffee. Note that the Coffee of the Day is usually not posted up on the main menu board. A sign is usually on the counter or near the regular-brew coffee machines.

In Summary

The basic menu seems easy enough to understand and to remember. You have:

- The basic *Espresso*, a 1 & ½ Oz. strongly brewed coffee.
- Espresso with a little frothed milk – *Espresso Macchiato*
- Espresso with whipped cream – *Espresso con Panna*
- A diluted espresso made by mixing a shot of espresso with hot water – an *Americano*
- The historic *Cappuccino,* made by most coffeehouses using a mixture of 1/3 espresso, 1/3 steamed milk, & 1/3 frothed milk.
- The American version of the *Latte*, usually 1 part espresso, and 3 to 5 parts steamed milk, and a small amount of foam on the top - various flavors.
- A chocolate version of the *Latte* or *Cappuccino* – a *Mocha* (drink ingredients vary by coffeehouse)

- The *Café Au Lait* that uses regular brewed coffee combined with an equal part of hot milk.
- And last, the *Coffee of the Day* which is the featured regular brewed coffee at the coffeehouse that day. (Note: Frequently coffeehouses will feature more than one *Coffee of the Day*.)

Simple enough! And having knowledge of these basic offerings will certainly go a long way in making you feel comfortable in any coffeehouse. In fact almost everyone who frequents coffeehouses has at one time or another been confused by coffee drink names. The problem is that we Americans like to customize everything including our coffee drinks. Smart business people who run coffeehouses, both independents and franchise owners cater to this desire and encourage it by offering numerous options. Coffeehouse drink offerings and coffeehouse culture, although having its roots from other parts of the world, have become uniquely American. Not since Ford started offering cars in different colors, other than black in the 1940's and the old Bell System started offering different colors of telephones in the 1950's (originally available around the world is black only), are there so many choices for the coffee drinker. Even Dell Computer could learn lessons from Starbucks on how to increase sales by customizing the product for the consumer.

See the *Coffee Fanatic's Coffee Drink Reference Chart* on the next page as a further reference.

Understanding Coffee Drinks

	Brewed Coffee	Espresso*	Steamed Milk[1]	Foamed Milk	Whip Cream	Hot Water	Sugar/ Sweetener	Garnishes[2]	Flavors
Latte		1/4	3/4	¼ inch	Opt.			C,N, or SC	Opt.
Cappuccino		1/3	1/3	1/3	Opt.				
Caffè Mocha		1/3	1/3		Opt.		Opt.	C,N, or SC	1-2 Ozs. Chocolate Syrup
Mocha Latte or Moccaccino		1/4	3/4	¼ inch or none	Opt.				1-2 Ozs. Chocolate Syrup
Americano		1-2 Shots				6 Ozs.			
Caffè Au Lait	1/2	1/2							
Espresso con Panna		1-2 Shots			Large Dollop			Unsweetened Cocoa	
Caffè Macchiato		1-2 Shots		¼ inch					

* Espresso is usually measured as a "shot" or 1&1/2 Ozs. [1]Milk Options – Whole, Skim, ½ & ½, and Soy
[2] Common Garnish Codes: C = Cinnamon N = Nutmeg SC = Sweetened Cocoa

Step 2. Interpreting the language of the natives

To illustrate why this step and our third step on ordering is necessary, let's look at the various ways that you can order and customized a Latte. Oh, you can definitely walk into a coffeehouse and simply say, "I'd like a Latte". You will get a Latte as described earlier in the chapter, probably in a tall cup (12 oz.) since you did not specify the size. It will be made from caffeinated coffee and regular milk.

1,843,200 Versions of a Latte

Hardly anyone wants a regular latte however, and through the innovation of coffeehouse entrepreneurs coupled with the demands of our coffee fanatic consumers, you don't have to. At a typical coffeehouse there are 1,843,200 ways to order a Latte. Don't believe it? Do the math and figure out the possible Latte drink combinations as we go trough the various options:

Size of Drink – 4 choices, <u>Small</u> (8 Oz. Cup), <u>Tall</u> (12 Oz. Cup), <u>Grande</u> (16 Oz. Cup), <u>Venti</u> (20 Oz. Cup)

Type of Cup - 2 Choices: "<u>for here</u>" or "<u>to go</u>" (with lid)

Temperature – 2 Choices: <u>Regular</u> (Hot) or <u>Iced</u>

Coffee – 3 choices <u>Caffeinated</u>, <u>Decaffeinated</u>, and <u>½ Caffeinated</u>

Milk - A minimum of 4 choices: <u>Regular Milk</u>, <u>Low Fat</u> <u>Skim Milk</u> and <u>Soy</u>

Frothed Milk - 4 choices: <u>None</u>, <u>Regular Amount</u>, <u>Extra</u>, <u>Less</u>

Whipped Cream - 4 choices: <u>None</u>, <u>Regular Amount</u>, <u>Extra</u>, <u>Less</u>

Espresso Shots – Basically 4 choices: <u>1</u>, <u>2</u>, <u>3</u>, or <u>4</u>

Sugar – 5 choices: <u>None</u>, <u>Regular Amount</u>, <u>Extra</u>, <u>Less</u> & <u>No-cal</u>

Flavors – Typically 10: <u>Almond</u>, <u>Caramel</u>, <u>Chocolate</u>, <u>Coconut</u>, <u>Hazelnut</u>, <u>Irish Cream</u>, <u>Mint</u>, <u>Raspberry</u>, and <u>Vanilla</u>

Garnishes – Typically 3: <u>Chocolate</u>, <u>Cinnamon</u>, and <u>Nutmeg</u>

Considering the other types of drinks the coffeehouses offer (and all their variations), there are easily over 5 million possible ordering combinations at the average café. It is no wonder that coffeehouses have developed their own lingo over time to clarify and speed up the ordering process; especially between the order-taker and the barista who is going to make the drink. While there is no official lexicon nevertheless code words have come into use to speed up the ordering process. Also, there are certainly differences between the major franchises and the independents as well as geographical differences concerning the terms used.

    To illustrate the use of this "coffee dictionary", let us suppose that you decide one day that you want to eliminate caffeine and cut back on whole milk. To help you over this change you also decide to order a bigger drink. Today you plan to get your coffee to go since you have been spending too much time at the coffeehouse lately. So instead of ordering your regular latte, today you walk in to your favorite coffeehouse and say, "I'll have a Grande latte with De-Caf and skim milk. No whip cream please and I'd also like Equal instead of sugar and can I have that to go?" The clerk shouts across the room to the barista, "1 Grande whipless skinny harmless with Cher sugar and legs." Skinny refers to skim milk, "harmless" means decaffeinated, and "legs" gets you a cup with lid to go.

Step 3. Ordering your drink correctly (Coffee House Lingo)

Should you use the correct coffeehouse terminology or continue to sound like a dweed? That's up to you, of course. The Coffee Fanatic's Field Guide strives to educate everyone so that they feel comfortable at any coffeehouse. We offer the Coffee Fanatic's *Ordering Dictionary* for your use and in the spirit of sharing. Regional variations withstanding, these terms are used in many coffeehouses and among baristas.

When specifying the number of espresso shots:
- Single 1&1/2 Oz. –*a solo*
- Two Shots –a *doppio*
- Three Shots - *a triple*
- Four Shots – *a quad*

When specifying the size of the drink:
- Small (8 Oz.) – *Small (also, Short)*
- Tall (12 Oz.) – *Tall (also, Alto)*

- Large (16 Oz.) – *Grande*
- Extra Large (20 Oz.) – *Venti*

Note: The number of different sizes offered do vary, and occasionally the terminology, so check the local menu before ordering

Terms for types of drinks:

Espresso with half caffeinated coffee – *a Split Shot*

Cappuccino – *a Cap*

- Cappuccino with less milk than normal – *a Dry Cap*
- Cappuccino with more milk than normal – *a Wet Cap*
- Cappuccino without frothed milk - *Without*

Lattes – In many big city coffeehouses, lattes are the assumed preference so the word latte frequently goes unspoken. Instead, terms to describe affiliation or type of milk are used. For example:

- Latte with skim milk - *a Skinny*
- Latte with soymilk – *a Soy*
- Latte with decaffeinated coffee – *a Harmless (also, No Fun)*
- Latte with both skim milk & decaf – *Why Bother (also, Skinny Harmless)*
- Latte with caramel flavoring – *a Caramel*

Regular Coffee – *a Drip*

- Regular Coffee of the Day – *COD*
- Regular Coffee, ½ caffeinated – a *Schizo*

- Regular brewed coffee with a shot of espresso – *a Red Eye, (also, Depth Charge, Hammerhead, Speed Ball, & a Shot in the Dark)*

Mochas
- ½ regular mocha & ½ white mocha – *a Zebra*
- Double tall mocha with whole milk & extra whipped cream – *Thunder Thighs*

Terms for the type of milk or sugar:
- Make with skim milk – *a Skinny*
- Double cream & double sugar – *Cake in a cup (also, a Double Double)*
- Espresso with ½ & ½ - *a Breve*
- Without frothed milk – *Foamless*
- With no-cal sugar – *Cher sugar*

Terms for the strength of the coffee:
- Decaffeinated coffee – *a Harmless (also, Unleaded & Virgin)*
- Half caffeinated & half decaffeinated – *a Half Caf*
- Caffeinated - *High-test*

Miscellaneous Terms:
- Coffee drink to go – *With Legs (also, With Wings, On Wheels, With Handles, & On a Leash)*
- Coffee drink to stay – *Park it*
- Without whipped cream – *Whipless*
- Add ice cubes to cool coffee drink – *Shock It*

Chapter 4 – Become a Coffee Barista In Your Own Home

(And Impress All Your Friends)

Field Guide Chapter 4 Highlights

- ➢ *How recognizing coffee tree species will help you brew a better cup*
- ➢ *Identifying world-wide coffee growing habitats*
- ➢ *Field Guide tips for purchasing and brewing coffee*
- ➢ *Understanding the differences between mass-roasted and specialty coffee beans*
- ➢ *Navigating the supermarket aisles and the coffee bins of roasters*

Almost everyone would like to make a better cup of coffee, both for their daily consumption and for those special occasions when they are entertaining friends. Many Coffee Fanatics use a few different coffees at home. Similar to wine connoisseurs, there is the coffee that they drink frequently (like a good table wine) and coffees, either regular brewed or espresso that they serve on special occasions or when friends are over the house. The wine connoisseur does not drink the $63. bottle of French Bordeaux every day and neither does the coffee aficionado have Jamaican Blue Mountain (about $40. per bag) frequently. Aside from the selection of the coffee that is similar to purchasing wine, coffee of course has to also be prepared. It has to be stored, ground when ready to be used (highly recommended), combined with water, brewed, and frequently other ingredients are added like milk, sugar, garnishes, etc.

Starting with the selection of the coffee itself, there are many steps along the way to sabotage what should be a smooth process, ending with a great tasting cup of coffee. Therefore, this chapter and the next one is dedicated to all those coffee drinkers who have tried numerous types of coffees and who have owned perhaps eighteen different coffee makers and still don't understand why their coffee does not taste like the coffee they buy outside the home or even that perfect cup that Aunt Sally serves. In the quest for better tasting coffee, a field guide is definitely needed to both identify the different coffees, understand packaging and marketing, and to navigate through the marketing quagmire aimed at us consumers.

Photo by Nadia Mercer

Of course there is a lot of advice already out there on making the "perfect cup" of coffee and how it can cure a lot of ills – and there always has been. The following is from *Dr. Chase's Recipes; or Information for Everybody* by A.W. Chase, M.D. – Fifteenth New and Enlarged Edition, copyright 1867. Published by R.A. Beal, Ann Arbor, Michigan.

> "**Soot Coffee** – Has cured many cases of Ague, after everything else has failed. It is made as follows: Soot scraped from a chimney, (that from stove-pipes does not

do,) 1 tablespoon, steeped in water 1 pt., and settled with 1 egg beaten up in a little water, as for other coffee, with sugar and cream, 3 times daily with the meals, in place of other coffee. It has come in very much to aid restoration in Typhoid Fever, bad cases of Jaundice, Dyspepsia, etc., etc."

I wonder how a Soot Latte would taste? At a typical coffeehouse today, you would probably order "A Grande Latte – Soot It!" Well to get on with our field-guide approach, let's start with the different coffee species and their regions of growth.

Coffee Plant Species and Regions of Growth
(What you need to know)

Coffee Plants thrive in tropical, mountainous climates with adequate rainfall. Only Hawaii in the United States has the proper climate for coffee trees. The resulting coffee is known as Kona, coming from the Kona region of Hawaii. 100% Kona is an excellent full-bodied coffee but watch out for the blends which can vary greatly in flavor (see the information and tips below on blended coffees.)

> **Note:** *For all you trivia fans, you can win a bet that there is another coffee tree in the USA, right in the heart of Middle America. It is not the same as the Arabica or Robusta species. It is known as The Kentucky Coffee Tree and the fruit are pods that are long and flat. The seeds from the pods were brewed by the early pioneers as coffee.*

Although many countries grow coffee, the top eight of world's largest producers of coffee, listed in order of volume are:

    1. Brazil
    2. Vietnam
    3. Columbia

4. Indonesia
5. Mexico
6. Ethiopia
7. Guatemala
8. India

Many other countries, while producing less volume than the top eight do produce some of the best coffee in the world. These are countries like **Costa Rica, El Salvador, Guatemala, Honduras, Kenya, Jamaica, New Guinea, Sumatra**, and the aforementioned **Hawaiian Kona** coffee.

While there are many species of coffee plants, the two that are grown for sale around the world are Arabica and Robusta. You will frequently see these terms on the coffee products that you are considering for purchase.

Above average coffee plants grow in tropical climates where temperature ranges between 60° to 90°F year round. Elevations vary from 1000 to 6000 feet (the higher, the better). Well-drained soil and abundant and regular rainfall are the other elements for a good coffee crop. Left alone, the coffee trees will grow to about 30 feet high. However, most of them are kept trim to 10 feet or lower to facilitate picking. Hybrid varieties, especially of the Arabica species have also been developed that both lessen the probably of disease and increase the quantity of the yield. After blooming, they bear a cherry like fruit, which contains two seeds that are the coffee beans.

In order for all of us to enjoy our cup of java, the coffee cherries need to be picked (in some climates, more than once a year) and the seeds (later to become coffee beans) need to be extracted. Various methods are used for extracting the seeds including drying the cherries and also, by soaking the cherries in water. Suffice it to say that these separation processes are very critical and if not done correctly, the flavor of the coffee will suffer. The seeds, at this point, called green coffee, are shipped to roasting plants around the world.

It also needs to be pointed out that the quality of the coffee crop each year is affected by an individual region's growing conditions, temperatures, amount of rainfall, etc. When you consider these factors along with the many steps along the way (i.e., the separating process used, the exporting process, the importing process, the roasting process used, the packaging, etc., is it any wonder that it is difficult to brew a consistently good tasting cup of coffee. One has more respect for the local coffeehouse when we realize this plus face our own responsibilities in brewing a cup for home consumption like grinding the beans, choosing the right water, storing the coffee and selecting the brewing equipment to use.

So, in our quest for serving a better cup of brew at home, we need to consider a few issues:

Issue 1 - Arabica or Robusta?

Arabica beans, photographed by Nadia Mercer

Of the two species of coffee plant, Arabica produces the better quality coffee with a more balanced, fuller flavor. While both are grown in the same areas of Central and South America, Africa, and Indonesia, Arabica plants are grown at higher altitudes (usually over 3000 feet), with almost constant rainfall and excellent soil drainage. Arabica comprises most of the good and excellent coffees of the world.

Robusta, grown at lower levels, on the other hand produces a lesser grade of coffee and is not as flavor able as Arabica. Incidentally, Robusta has almost twice the caffeine as Arabica. It is predominately used for instant coffees and various blends. Although Robusta is a necessary ingredient in roasting some of the above average espresso blends since it adds to the density of the crema (the mild foam-like topping on a cup of espresso).

Coffee Fanatic's Tip 1:

One key to making good coffee is to make sure that you always buy 100% Arabica beans. This fact should be labeled clearly on the coffee package.

Issue 2 - 100% Columbian or the Others?

As previously pointed out coffee is grown in many regions of the world but many of your everyday coffees that you will consider for purchase will be labeled **100% Columbian**. As mentioned in Chapter 1, back in 1960, the *Juan Valdez* advertising campaign has elevated Columbian coffee to a "Good Housekeeping Seal of Approval" status. Generally speaking, you can count on any coffee that you purchase labeled *100% Columbian* to be consistent and of good quality despite what you might have heard or read about elsewhere. Columbia produces over 10% of the world's coffee and is one of the top three producers of coffee in the world. The coffee is from the Arabica plant and is mostly grown at high altitudes. The Colombian Coffee federation has organized the nation's growers into a cohesive unit growing quality coffee according to precise standards. Based on an American national consumer organization's ratings study in 2004, the 100% Columbian and Columbian Supremo (highest grade of Columbian) varieties were rated the best. A Columbian coffee has similar attributes to some of the best specialty coffees.

Coffee Fanatic's Tip 2:

100% Columbian coffee offers excellent Arabica beans with a strong, full-bodied flavor at a very reasonable price. Like a good "table" wine consider it for everyday drinking.

Issue 3 - Specialty or Commercial Coffees?

Specialty Coffee is strictly an American term coined by Erna Knutsen, a coffee industry buyer and specialist in 1974. The term is the hallmark of identification for the specialty coffee industry and the Specialty Coffee Association of America (SCAA). Unfortunately, you will not find the term on any coffee bag. So, what is specialty coffee? Various coffee experts define it in different ways. The most common definition is that it is the exact opposite of blended

Commercial Coffee – it is not pre-packaged coffee, either ground or instant that we are accustomed to seeing on the supermarket shelves. Specialty coffee is definitely 100% Arabica from various parts of the world, and is frequently the highest grades and quality available in those regions.

To confuse consumers even more, specialty coffees are sometimes identified as "Gourmet" or "single-origin" coffees. Many feel that the "single-origin" label which specifies the country or region the coffee comes from is a better identifier than the word, "specialty." Although, as previously discussed, 100% Columbian is certainly "single–origin" but I am sure purists do not consider it in the same class as the rest of the specialty coffees. (Flavored coffees add another layer of confusion for consumers as they can be made from either specialty or blended coffees.) Unlike commercial coffees, specialty coffees are frequently roasted on the premises of a local Roaster to fill a specific customer order. Approximately 10% of coffeehouses roast right on the premises offering the maximum degree of coffee freshness to their customers. Specialty coffees are also sold to various other coffeehouses, high-end supermarkets, and natural food stores around the country. The specialty coffee industry can certainly claim a large role in the success and popularity of coffeehouses both in the drinks that they serve and the coffee that they sell to their customers.

All that being said, specialty coffee unfortunately does not have a clear product identification or differentiation in the marketplace. Except for people who are extremely knowledgeable about coffees, an average consumer scanning the shelves of a major supermarket chain, a Whole Foods Store or a Harris Teeter's can not really differentiate between many quality specialty coffees and commercial coffees. To complicate things even further, known specialty coffee companies like Starbucks, and Seattle's Best (now owned by Starbucks) are competing heavily in the commercial marketplace, even selling ground coffee (blasphemy to a specialty coffee purist) on the supermarket shelves right next to Maxwell House, Folgers, Hills Brothers, and Yuban. And at the same time, commercial coffee companies are venturing into the specialty coffee part of the market.

Because specialty coffee is not produced in the quantities of commercial coffee, it is usually twice the cost or more. People in the industry like to point out that specialty coffee is cheap and quote the per-cup cost which is very reasonable compared to buying a cup outside the home.

Coffee Fanatic's Tip 3

To be sure that you are getting "specialty" coffee, always buy it from your local coffeehouse where you can ask questions about the various types, when they were roasted, etc.

(See the chart at the end of this chapter for some "Specialty" recommendations)

Issue 4 - Blended coffee or a single-origin?

Today, even specialty coffee roasters are developing their own blends of coffee. You should be aware that all roasters, both big and small are motivated to blend coffee from different countries or regions for the following reasons: One, to improve upon the two individual coffees (the old, "the result is greater than the sum of the individual parts" theory). Or two, to lower costs by blending a cheaper coffee with a more expensive one. There are some excellent blended coffees out there where a roaster has skillfully blended together the strong attributes of two different coffees and in the process, canceled out the negative or not so favorable ones. Your local coffee shop owner or barista is a good source of information on local blends and the coffeehouse is an excellent place to sample them. But, as you look at a blended coffee on the supermarket's or retailer's shelf, how can you tell what the original reason for blending was? You can't and therefore, unless you have tasted the blend before, stay with single-origin coffees including the 100% Columbian.

Coffee Fanatic's Tip 4

Unless you have tasted the blended coffee in the past, don't buy it!

Issue 5 – What about the roast?

The roasting process is one of the most critical steps for coffee beans to reach their full flavor potential. As mentioned earlier in the chapter, after the coffee seeds are separated from the pulp and skin of the coffee cherries, they are dried and shipped to roasters around the world. Roasting these green seeds too long (very dark) or not long enough (very light) will significantly change the taste and acidity of the coffee. Both commercial and independent Roasters strive to roast their beans in accordance with the characteristic of the particular coffees. For example, they would not take a 100% Colombian Supremo or an Ethiopian Yirgacheffe and do a "light" or "medium" roast of the beans.

For the consumer, knowing the type of roast indicates basic information about the coffee's taste, body, and aroma. But like other facets of the coffee industry, there are no standards or even common terminology of the various roast types. This is not only true in America but also, around the world. Different coffee companies further complicate the understanding of their different coffees by having the marketing department name their different roasts. It is probably good for their sales but it certainly makes it difficult to compare roasts between the various brands.

Despite the different names and types of roasts that coffee companies use to make you think that you will taste an exotic coffee, there are only three basic roasts under which practically all coffees can be classified:

Light, Medium or Dark

There are gradations of roast levels within each category, and because of a lack of standards, one roaster's "dark" for example may be designated "medium" by another roaster. Most coffeehouse owners and employees however attempt to accurately classify their coffees as either "light, medium, dark" or "mild, average, strong."

The roast type tells you about the taste of the resulting coffee after the beans are brewed: There may be more eloquent and precisely correct ways of explaining the outcomes of the roasting process (In fact, books have been written on the subject – see Section III – Recommended Resources at the end of this book). However, a basic explanation of the three roast types that will help you in selecting coffees are as follows:

Light – means a smooth, balanced taste (not strong) with a pleasant aroma. The beans are light brown in color with no visible oil on their surface.

Medium – means a standard, more favorable taste with a solid aroma. The resulting beans tend to be a darker brown but with still no trace of coffee oil.

Dark – means a strong, full-bodied taste with an intense aroma. The resulting beans are usually dark brown, boarding on black in color and slightly oily.

In addition to the three basic types, other common roast classifications that you will come across are:

French Roast – Roasted longer than the typical Dark roast, the resulting coffee beans are very oiling and look black in color.

Italian Roast – This is a very dark roast similar to the French roast. There are no industry roasting standards and the words Italian or French are often chosen for their marketing affect to describe a company's darkest roast.

Vienna Roast – Slightly darker than "dark" roasts, but lighter than French or Italian roasts. The resulting beans are somewhat oiling and appear to be almost chocolate brown in color.

Espresso Roast – Roasted similarly to the Vienna roast, espresso coffee is usually made up of blended coffees including Robusta. Blending coffees for a good espresso roast is almost an art form. The proper mix of Robusta beans is actually desired as it results in a thicker and richer crema.

Coffee Fanatic's Tip 5

Become aware of the various types of roasts and how they affect the aroma, acidity, body & flavor relative to the way you like your coffee. Realize that the same roast can be labeled differently by the various companies.

Issue 6 – Time considerations in purchasing & brewing

Before you venture to the local market or coffeehouse to purchase your coffee for home consumption, you need to be aware of the time considerations that have ruined many a home brew. As a further obstacle to making a good cup of coffee at home, you need to know that coffee beans start loosing their flavor immediately after they are roasted. Furthermore, once they are grinded, they loose their flavor even quicker. And if that isn't enough to drive you to rent a room above the coffeehouse, once the coffee is brewed, the flavor loss continues at an even fastest rate than the first two steps.

Time Considerations In Enjoying Your "Cup of Joe"	
Type of Processing	*Considerable Flavor Is Lost After*
After Beans Are Roasted	2 Weeks
After The Coffee Is Ground	1 Hour
After The Coffee Is Brewed	15 Minutes

In terms of pre-roasted and pre-ground coffee, considerable steps can be taken (and are taken) to preserve the freshness of coffee during each stage of processing. As mentioned in Chapter 1, starting in 1985, major coffee roasters started using a one-way freshness valve that preserves the freshness of coffee beans and ground coffee (until the bag is opened) for up to nine months. Once you open this type of bag or buy freshly roasted coffee beans in a regular bag from your local coffeehouse, you should store your beans in a vacuum-sealed steel container immediately. It should be kept in a cool place but contrary to what you may have heard from your Mother, not in the refrigerator. While the refrigerator temperature will help keep the beans fresh, you run the risk of musty orders from stored food products contaminating the coffee flavor. Of course once the coffee is brewed, a good thermos type coffee pot (see Chapter 5) will keep your brewed coffee fresh and hot for a longer time than 15 minutes.

Coffee Fanatic's Tip 6

As a general rule, don't buy more coffee than you plan to use in the next week or so. Don't grind your coffee until you are ready to brew it. Only brew your coffee when you know you are ready to drink and serve it.

Navigating the Coffee Section of the Local Market

(A Coffee Fanatic's guide to purchasing the right coffees)

Whether you will be shopping in a coffeehouse that also roasts coffee on the premises (highly recommended for your better specialty coffees) or at a supermarket, our guide on the last page of this chapter will help you select the various coffees for brewing at home. Additionally I designed this guide in recognition of the fact that people these days purchase different types of coffees for their use. With coffee being grown in over 75 countries of the world, half of which are available in the United States, the choices are truly mind-boggling. Add to that the 400 or so commercial brands marketed in the US, not to mention the blends and roasts within each company's offerings. It is impossible to have a compressive chart covering every one of these possibilities. What the guide does is offer you some solid recommendations for brewing better coffee at home. It is a starting point to purchasing the right coffee based on your needs and taste preferences. We recommend you also explore the books and websites listed in our Section 3 Appendix of resources if you are interested in learning more.

> **Note:** *I recommend a number of "Every-Day" coffees depending upon the type of roast that you may like as well as whether you take it black or with milk and sugar. If you take only a slight amount of milk or sugar, you may want to stick with our "black" recommendations. For those of you who use a lot of milk and/or sugar, there is frankly no point in buying a more expensive coffee than a standard supermarket brand frequently labeled "100% Coffee." This coffee usually contains a blend of coffee beans, consisting mostly of the Robusta species. (The same is true for iced coffee drinks.) The milk and sugar mask a lot of shortcomings of the coffee itself. You may want to do some comparison tests on your own to see if you can tell the difference between the better coffees and the "100% coffee" blends.*

Some Notes About Coffee Labels

Coffee labels look simple and clear enough to read. However they are deceptive in what they do not say. There is no standardization in the coffee industry so it is strictly a "buyer beware" situation. For example, some companies indicate the type of roast and others use a marketing term like "Dinner Blend" which means absolutely nothing. Looking at the first 5 issues mention earlier in the chapter, here is what you can tell, sometimes, from the label:

Arabica or Robusta? Whenever a company is using Arabica (You will recall, the better of the two species.) they will always state so proudly and prominently on the label "***100% ARABICA BEANS.*** Otherwise the label will say something like, "***100% Coffee***" or "***Our Special*** (fill in the blank) **Coffee."**

100% Columbian or the Others? Colombian coffee is comprised of 100 % Arabica beans but some companies will just use the term, *"100% COLOMBIAN"* on the label since they feel it is a more recognizable term to the average consumer.

Specialty or Commercial Coffees? As mentioned, always buy specialty coffee at your local coffeehouse or coffeehouse/roaster. There, you can ask questions to a knowledge person about the coffees, when they were roasted, type of roast, characteristics, etc. Specialty coffees are not labeled as such at the supermarket. Do not think that you are buying true specialty coffee at the supermarket because in has a known specialty company's label on it.

Blended coffee or a single-origin? The simple rule here is that unless you have tasted and enjoyed a blended coffee in the past, stay away from any coffee that has the word *"Blend"* on the label unless you are planning to use it for iced coffee drinks or you use a lot of milk and sugar as our chart suggests. Blends are the same as the term, *"100% Coffee"* – it doesn't tell you anything about the different types of coffees used.

What about the roast? Our chart indicates the three main roasts. Labels will use similar terms. Be aware that some companies will use marketing terms, like, "Rich" for dark or "Original" which usually means a Medium roast. Still other companies will add more levels in the roasting spectrum. For example, instead of Dark, they will have both Medium-Dark and Dark. Because of no coffee labeling standards, you need to convert marketing terminology to the three basic types to facilitate purchasing a roast that you may enjoy.

Some Notes About the Packaging

Pre-packaged or container coffee will always indicate whether the beans are Whole Bean or Ground. It is recommended that you purchase whole bean coffee rather than ground coffee since it is fresher. In buying whole bean coffee, practically all reputable coffee companies will remove the oxygen before sealing their bags plus the bags will contain those button-sized, one-way valves. The purpose of these valves is to dissipate the carbon dioxide that is being released as a result of the roasting process. These valves, invented about 35 years ago have contributed greatly to the freshness of our brew. <u>Coffee roasters will normally date the bag by printing or stamping a "use-by" date on their packages.</u> Note: Coffee companies don't agree on the length of time the coffee beans will stay fresh in this type of bag. That is why you will find some dates a year into the future.

Coffee Fanatic's Tip 7

Resist buying coffee from coffee bins in various retail stores unless the roasted dates are clearly posted. You may be buying stale coffee.

Purchase Recommendations for Use At Home

Coffee Recommendations	Every-Day Coffee (Milk&Sugar)	Every-Day Coffee (Black)	Espresso Drinks	Special Occasions Mild	Special Occasions Medium	Special Occasions Dark	Iced Coffee Drinks
100% Coffee	✓						✓
100% Colombian	✓						
Colombian Supremo		✓					
100% Arabica		✓					
French or Italian Roast		✓					
Espresso Roast			✓				
Costa Rican Tarrazu					✓		
Ethiopian Yirgacheffe					✓	✓	
Guatemalan Antigua				✓	✓		
Jamaican Blue Mtn.				✓	✓		
Kenya AA					✓		
Hawaiian Kona				✓			
Sumatran Mandheling						✓	
Yemen Mocha					✓		

Chapter 5 – The Strange World Of Coffee Makers

From Pre-historic to Modern Species

Field Guide Chapter 5 Highlights

> ➢ *Appreciating the need for more than one coffee maker*
> ➢ *Understanding the older species and their advantages*
> ➢ *Selecting the newer species along with the right features*
> ➢ *Field Guide tips and "Impressive Values" for selecting coffee makers to match your lifestyle*

Indeed, a Strange World

Coffee makers or coffee pots have come in a variety of sizes and shapes throughout America's history. Indeed many of them are strange looking like the antique vacuum coffee maker pictured on the previous page (top left depiction). Even today, the large variety of the newer Pod coffeemakers have a "Starwars" like quality to their design (bottom right). In addition to normal differences based on brewing methods, the major manufacturers add to the confusion by making so many variations of the same type of coffee maker. A recent visit to Mr. Coffee's website uncovered no less than sixty nine models of an automatic drip coffee maker. They make from 1-cup models to 45-cup models, offer different carafes, different programmable features, and of course, different colors. In this chapter, we will take a look at identifying and selecting the right coffee maker (or makers) to suit your needs.

Identifying & Selecting
(Practical or Impressive)

There is both a practical approach and an entertaining approach to selecting coffee makers. Like our coffee recommendations, you may want to consider selecting both paths: one for every day brewing and one for entertaining or for those special occasions. There are so many brands and types of Coffee Makers that we could have a whole field guide on their identification, nomenclature and how to navigate the store shelves in search of a suitable one. Of course my purpose is to educate the average person so that they are not a one-dimensional coffee geek: who only stands in line at the coffeehouse and orders his or her latte. My desire is that all Coffee Fanatics become skilled in brewing a good cup of coffee or a cappuccino at home especially when they want to impress their friends.

There are so many good choices in Coffee Makers these days that do their job close to perfection that as long as you do a good job in selecting the coffee (See Chapter 4) you are 90% along the way to impressing your friends with your own brew at home. The conveniences and features of today's coffee makers are overwhelming compared to what your grandmother used (a peculator pot that heated the coffee to boiling and spoiled the flavor in the process) or going back even further, the "cowboy" brewing method of cooking the raw coffee beans over the open fire.

Coffee purists have their own preferences. They tend to shun the modern conveniences and features and favor the old fashion coffee pots and brewing methods. They have convinced themselves and each other that these older methods produce better tasting coffee. In the past, they have had a convincing argument but current manufacturers have made greatly improved products that coupled with the convenience of operating them, far outweigh the older brewing methods.

Of course brewing quality espresso properly at home is difficult to do for the average consumer and the equipment is expensive. Your best option for true espresso, unless you are willing to spend a lot of money is still your favorite coffeehouse.

Interesting enough, some of these older methods do produce a good cup of coffee and using them are excellent ways of impressing your friends when you are entertaining. So for both informational purposes as well as entertainment possibilities, let us look at the older, basic methods for brewing a cup of coffee.

The Older Species
The Manual Drip Maker

Basically the same as an automatic drip Mr. Coffee, this maker is the least expensive of all the methods. You simply need a coffee filter holder that you place on top of your cup or carafe (they are available in different sizes. Add the filter and the coffee grounds. You then heat the water separately and pour it over the grounds.

Advantages A superior cup of coffee – especially if the water is heated properly (about 200°F – not boiling) and it is added to the grounds at proper intervals, you can brew a perfect cup. Also coffee fanatics who like to load up on the coffee grounds for an exceptionally strong brew (you can not always do this with an automatic coffee maker as the water will overflow if there are too many grounds in the filter.

Disadvantages It can be a major inconvenience and a number of chances for fouling up the process exist. For example, you can add the water too fast so that the grounds do not get saturated properly. Or you can go too slowly (the water should normally mix with the grounds for about 5 minutes) and the flavor will suffer.

Today's modern automatic drip coffee makers have solved the problems of this manual method as: they heat the water to the proper temperature and then brew the coffee for the right amount of time (see the write-up on *The Automatic Drip Coffee Maker* later in this chapter)

Impressive Value* – *None In fact there should probably be a negative value assigned since you will be embarrassed if your friends see you using this method and spilling hot water all over yourself. You'll only make it worse if you try to explain that you are really making a superior cup of coffee.

Coffee Fanatic's Tip 8
Stay away from the Manual Drip Maker method unless you can't afford an automatic coffee maker.

The French Press

This is essentially a glass pot with a plunger. The coffee grounds are place in the pot first. Then you pour the hot water (just short of boiling water – about 200°F). Allow the grounds to saturate the water for about 4 minutes. Operate the plunger slowly but firmly separating the brewed coffee from the grounds.

Advantages The French Press produces a thicker richer flavor than other methods. Extracting more flavors out of the coffee grounds, it is particularly suggested for drinkers of decaffeinated coffee.

Disadvantages The coffee grinds, especially the finer particles, frequently mix with the brewed coffee, giving it a graining taste. Also, it may produce too strong a cup for your average every day coffee drinker. The coffee cools quickly so it has to be enjoyed immediately. Lastly, the French Press is time consuming to clean properly.

Coffee Fanatic's Impressive Value – High While the French Press is not for every-day use, you can make serving after dinner coffee into quite an event, brewing it right in front of everyone at the table. Most people have not seen a French

Photo by Nadia Mercer

Press before. Your reputation as a chef and connoisseur is sure to rise. And let's be realistic – people aren't going to remember so much the taste of the coffee weeks afterwards (unless it was completely horrible) as they will remember the elegant and unique way that you brewed it.

Coffee Fanatic's Tip 9

Use a coarser grind so it will not clog up the plunger or pass through to the coffee after pressing. Depending upon your guests, you may want to get a milder roast than usual to counteract the effects of the brewing process. Do a practice run before the big event so everything comes off smooth.

Coffee Fanatic's Tip 10

French Presses are hard to find except from your local coffeehouse. I find that many coffeehouses sell them and the owners are also an excellent source of information on the type of coffee to use with them.

The Neapolitan Drip

Originally invented by the French in the early 1800's, this pot was adopted by the Italians and has been used by them ever since. This pot is also known as a Flip pot. The brewing unit is really two pots; one pot, upside down, is placed on top of another pot, right side up. In between the two pots is a filter where the coffee is placed. The water is placed in the bottom pot and the whole contraption is heated on the stove. When the water boils, the pot is grasped by both handles and flipped over allowing the water to drip through the filter.

Advantages These pots make excellent coffee.

Disadvantages Brewing regular coffee in this pot will result in a brew with a higher degree of bitterness compared to coffee brewed in an automatic drip maker.

Coffee Fanatic's Tip 11

The trick to making a good cup of coffee with a Neapolitan Drip pot is to catch the water either right at the start of the boil or just before the process begins. That way the water will not be too hot when you flip it and the coffee will be more favorable.

Neapolitan Drip pot – Photo by Nadia Mercer

The Vacuum Coffee Maker

This coffee maker consists of a large carafe on the bottom and a large glass vessel on the top. Water is placed in the carafe and the coffee grounds are poured into the top vessel. The whole contraption is then placed over heat. Once the water starts to boil, it is forced into the upper vessel. The coffee grinds and water are then manually stirred to facilitate the brewing process. Next, after approximately three minutes, the pot is removed from the heat, a vacuum occurs and the brewed coffee is sucked through the filter into the lower carafe.

Advantages Makes an excellent cup of coffee. And unlike the French Press, the Vacuum coffee maker produces a smooth tasting coffee free of any fine particles or grit.

Disadvantages It is an archaic way off making your daily coffee, awkward to use and time consuming to clean.

Impressive Value – <u>**High**</u> Like the French Press the vacuum coffee maker is not for every-day use but it is excellent for impressing even your most ardent coffee connoisseur friends by brewing coffee right in front of them. This is accomplished by getting the tabletop model (many coffeehouses sell them) that allows you to control the heat right where everyone is gathered around after dinner. It is quite a culinary event when the vacuum occurs in the lower carafe and the coffee is both heard and seen being sucked down into it.

The Stovetop Espresso Maker

The stovetop espresso maker offers you a reasonable and affordable way to enjoy every-day espresso at home. This brewer is also known as a Macchinetta. It makes espresso through boiling water creating steam that forces the water from the bottom chamber by pushing it upward and through the coffee grinds. This process of pushing the hot water quickly through the coffee grinds gives you that extra strong coffee that you do not get from drip methods.

Advantages While it is not the same quality as the espresso at your favorite coffeehouse, it will produce a reasonably textured, strong and smooth drink.

Disadvantages

While you can get a practical every-day espresso for drinking at home, there is no capability of frothing milk for cappuccinos or lattes. Additionally the brewing process does not produce that crema that forms on the top of a true espresso.

Impressive Value – Medium After all, you will be using this pot on the stove so no mileage is gained from the brewing process itself like with that of the Vacuum maker or Neapolitan brewers. However some of your friends may be impressed with your espresso especially if you serve it properly. (Also, see the tip below which can change the value to "High".)

Stovetop Espresso Maker- Photo by Nadia Mercer

Coffee Fanatic's Tip 12

If you like your cappuccinos or lattes at home now and then, an alternate to buying an expensive professional espresso maker is to use the stovetop espresso maker with a separate milk steamer. Then you will have all the ingredients to make a first class drink.

The Percolator

Many of the older Coffee Fanatics recall the percolator coffee pot more that any other type. This is because up until about 1980, it was the primary coffee pot used in American homes. Essentially the water is brought to a boil and forced up the center cylinder of the filter basket holder. It is then pushed out over the coffee grinds and filters through the basket to the bottom of the pot only to be circulated again to the top of the cylinder. Frequently people didn't keep track of how long the coffee brewed on the stovetop, sometimes resulting in the top being blown off and coffee spilling all over the stove. The brewing process also made for a very strong and bitter coffee with little aroma. The invention of the electric model only improved the taste slightly as it controlled the temperature of the water better.

The Pot Method

The open pot method is an uncomplicated old fashion method of adding the coffee grounds to hot water. That is until it is time to drink the brew. After the water comes close to boiling, the coffee grinds are added. The blend is then stirred for about 3 minutes. Once the coffee is brewed, some purists will wait for the grinds to settle and then carefully pour the coffee while others will pour the coffee through a strainer. A lot of potential problems exist such as knowing when the water is hot enough, having the proper coarseness of the grind, knowing the correct length of time to stir the mixture and of course separating the grinds from the brewed coffee. Needless to say, the coffee winds up either weak or strong and all possible degrees in between.

Cold Water Brewing

This method is certainly a conversational starter but the quality of the coffee is questionable. The main advantage to this method is that you wind up with coffee that is low in acidity. This is because cold water brewing extracts less fatty acids and oils, resulting in a 70% reduction of acidity. However, the coffee will not be as strong or favorable as with traditional brewing methods. It is well worth trying if you have to cut back on acid because of stomach problems. I would recommend using coffee that is a darker roast than what you normally like in order to compensate for the milder brew.

A pound of coffee is usually brewed at once by steeping the coffee in 8 to 10 cups of cold water for about 12 hours. The resulting brew is then filtered and is stored in the refrigerator. The brewed and stored concentrated coffee is then added to hot water (2 Ozs. for every 6 Ozs. of hot water. Although you can buy a specific coffee pot for this method (See Recommended Resources in Section III), you can also brew it in a regular pot as long as you can filter out the grinds when finished.

The Newer Species

The Automatic Drip Coffee Maker

Let us face it – the automatic drip coffee maker is the top choice for most Coffee Fanatics for brewing coffee at home. And for a couple of good reasons:

1. Coffee Fanatics drink a lot of coffee
2. Coffee Fanatics lead a busy life

On most days, we don't have time for other time consuming coffee brewing methods that are cumbersome to use and time consuming to prepare and clean up. We are willing to sacrifice some quality for time and convenience. And as it turns out, we are really not sacrificing a lot of quality. A recent Consumer Reports article found over 20 brands and models to be "very good" for brewing coffee. Of that number, 9 were judged to be "excellent".

Chapter 5 The Strange World of Coffee Makers - 83

With this type of electric drip maker, water is first heated to a boil similar to a percolator to force it up and through the filter basket. But unlike a percolator, once the water is forced to the top of the drip maker, it is sprayed over the grinds that are in the filter basket and the brewed coffee is dripped to the carafe below. During this brewing/drip process the water is between 195°F & 200°F and the coffee is brewed in only about 3-4 minutes so you don't get the over extraction of flavor that takes place during the percolating process. The filter basket can either hold a disposable paper filter or a permanent mesh filter (typically gold-plated). The carafe can also vary from glass to an insulated thermos type. In addition they come with a variety of features to customize the strength and quality of the brew plus to make your life easier.

Ever since Joe DiMaggio started appearing on our television sets in the 1970's to convince us to switch from a percolator to an electric automatic drip coffee maker (Joe was the spokesperson for Mr. Coffee), automatic drips have become by far the most widely used coffee maker in America. With its many

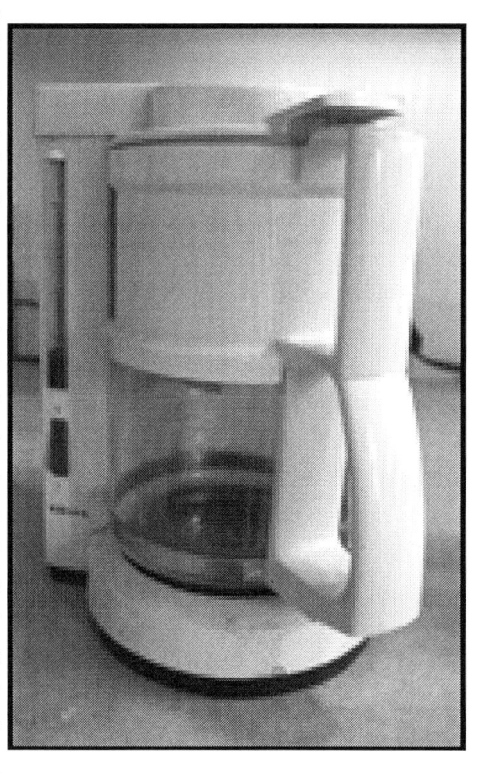

Photo by Nadia Mercer

features and conveniences, it is hard to surpass. The automatic drop coffee maker is also constantly being improved. Mr. Coffee alone has close to 70 models to satisfy the different cup capacities, carafe types, and other features that American consumers demand. The other major manufactures like Braun, Cuisinart, Farberware, Hamilton Beach, Krups, Proctor Silex, etc. are all fighting for market share, and the American consumer is the beneficiary.

Advantages These brewers make an excellent cup of coffee. Also in selecting an automatic drip coffee maker, you are eliminating a major source of problems in getting a good cup of coffee – the brewing process. Assuming that you purchase and grind good coffee beans, you can consistently brew a good to excellent pot with the strength that you like every time. Convenience, speed of brewing and ease of cleaning are also key advantages.

Disadvantages <u>None</u> - Although a lot of coffee purists have snubbed their noses at the automatic drip coffee makers, these days most of their objections to this brewing method have been resolved. For example, today's modern automatic drip coffee makers have solved the past problems of not heating the water to the proper temperature. Additionally past models took almost twice as long to brew (over 10 minutes) which over extracted flavor from the coffee beans resulting in a more bitter taste. That is no longer the case as most models brewing after about 5 minutes. After brewing, the old coffee makers ruined the flavor with the hot plate devices that were used to keep the coffee at the proper temperature. With current models, the warming devices are more accurately controlled or you can eliminate the problem entirely by getting a thermos carafe to store the brewed coffee in.

Impressive Value – <u>Generally low</u> since you are brewing the coffee in your kitchen. Some of your friends may be impressed with the features that you have or if you got one of the newer models that are color-coordinated with all your other counter-top appliances (mixer, toaster, etc.)

Coffee Fanatic's Tip 13

The automatic drip is the coffee maker that is going to sustain most of us Coffee Fanatics on a day-to-day basis. Therefore it is important to get a good one and one that has the features that will help us enjoy our favorite drink. These coffee makers come with an overabundance of features but here are some of the key ones that most Coffee Fanatics should get:

1. Spend a few more bucks and get a **thermal carafe** with your coffee maker. This will make that second cup so much more enjoyable compared to the hotplate type heaters that ruin the flavor of the coffee by overheating it after it is brewed.

2. If, at times, you are only going to brew a cup or two get a coffee maker with a **small batch setting**. This feature moderates the strength of the water flow through the grinds for just a couple of cups, resulting in a more balanced brew than models primarily designed for 8 to 12 cups.

3. Get a coffee maker that is **programmable** especially if time is limited in the morning. You will need to grind the coffee the night before but this is okay if you add milk as it will tend to mask any deterioration of the coffee grinds that occurred over night. If you take your coffee black and strong, then you can always get a combination grinder and coffee maker. With such a model, you can program it to grind and brew shortly before you get out of bed.

4. Another great feature if you need to get out of your place in a hurry, is to get a coffee maker where you can brew right into a **thermos coffee mug** that is made to fit right under the brewer (or better yet the double mug model if you need 2 cups to get going in the morning).

The Pod Coffee Maker

Like many new car models, these relatively new coffee makers will only improve over time. Initially imported from Europe by Philips, practically every coffee maker manufacturer now has a stylish looking Pod brewer. Essentially these coffee makers forced the heated water through a tea bag-like packet of ground coffee. The basic models only make 1 cup while the more expensive ones can brew two cups. While this coffee maker could be ideal for people living by themselves, it is currently not suitable for most Coffee Fanatics. Unlike an automatic drip coffee maker where we typically double the amount of water and coffee for our normal mug size, with Pod brewers you are stuck with only a European sized cup (about 6 ounces). In addition, the types and varieties of coffees that you need to purchase in pre-ground packets are currently limited.

Coffee Fanatic's Tip 14

Don't get roped in by the sleek design, the different colors that are offered, and the sophisticated marketing campaigns. If you think that you may want a pod coffee maker, try one out a friend's house first before making an investment. Also be aware that in recent coffee maker evaluations, they were not found to make

a better cup of coffee compared to automatic drip makers.

Other Coffee Makers

As stated at the start of this chapter, there are numerous types of coffee makers. Some older models have been replaced by newer more efficient coffee makers and others are just not that convenient to use for the average coffee drinker. However some Coffee Fanatics may want to explore some of these coffee makers and/or brewing methods that are still in use today, albeit by fewer and fewer people. Some of the books and other resources in Section III offer a great deal of information about these methods.

"Coffee should be black as hell, strong, as death, and sweet as love." Ancient Turkish saying

Should you consider coffee above sex?

After all, every Coffee Fanatic knows:

1. Great coffee is always available, even at work!
2. You can make a cup of coffee last for as long as you want to.
3. You can safely have coffee with a complete stranger.
4. Coffee is always gratifying.
5. You can be tied, sick, or not in the mood – plus individual performance is never an issue!
6. You will not feel guilty about having coffee when your spouse is not around.
7. You can enjoy coffee no matter how old you are.
8. A headache is never an excuse for not having coffee!
9. You can enjoy coffee anywhere, anytime you want.
10. You will never catch a disease or become pregnant.
11. You will not feel guilty the next day.

Chapter 6 – Putting It All Together

(To Serve a Great Cup of Coffee)

Field Guide Chapter 6 Highlights

- ➢ *It starts with proper storage*
- ➢ *The significance of good water*
- ➢ *Avoiding various pitfalls*
- ➢ *The power of the presentation!*

In Chapter 4, we covered the different types of coffees for brewing at home and in Chapter 5, we recommended the brewing equipment. Now that you have purchased just the right type of coffee beans from an exotic part of the world and have a first class coffee maker, what else can possibly go wrong in brewing a good cup of coffee when you have your friends over? – PLENTY!

Nevertheless, in this chapter, I will show you how to avoid these pitfalls and guide you through the process of actually brewing coffee at home to achieve two goals:

A. Impress all your friends by serving them a memorable cup of coffee.

B. Enjoy a better cup of coffee at home – every day!

Before we discuss the actual brewing and serving of an impressive cup of coffee, there are four important details to carry out:

1. Storing the Coffee at Home

Nothing can kill an enjoyable evening like a stale cup of coffee. As you will recall from Chapter 4, if you buy freshly roasted beans, they will loose considerable flavor after two weeks. In addition, once you open a vacuum-sealed bag of coffee beans, this rapid deterioration process begins. So only buy enough coffee that you plan to use in the near term. In addition, once you get the coffee home, if it has not been properly sealed (ask the shop owner if you are not sure) you need to store it in an airtight container that is perfectly dry. Use your coffee within two weeks. Keep the coffee in a cool place but not in your refrigerator. There are just too many odors in a typical refrigerator that can ruin the flavor of your coffee. In addition, there is the strong possibility of moisture getting into your coffee beans and spoiling them.

Coffee Fanatic's Tip 15:

When you bring coffee beans home, there are four elements of nature that stand in your way of having a great cup of coffee:

    a. Dampness

    b. Air

    c. Light

    d. Hot Temperatures

So, store your coffee in a dry, airtight & stainless steel container. Keep them in a cool, dark place like a pantry or closed door cabinet.

2. The Water

Water is almost 99% of you cup of coffee so it is a critical ingredient. Follow this simple rule: *If you currently do not like the way your glass of water tastes or smells it is not going to make a good cup of coffee!*

Many coffee aficionados recommend using cold water and this Coffee Fanatic does too. This is because cold tap water is fresher than hot water (especially if you let it run for a few minutes) – it is unlikely that you will pick up any off tastes or odors from the pipes that could affect the overall flavor of your brewed coffee. Here in Virginia where I live there is sulfur in the water that gives off a rotten-egg odor to the hot water. The cold water however is okay.

Some experts argue that cold water from either wells of city water systems contain many organic compounds and certain minerals that play havoc with the brewing process. Older homes, apartments, and certain city water systems for example, may also contain minor amounts of rust or different sediments. These experts recommend either in-house water filtration systems or using bottled spring water to brew your coffee.

The best approach is to experiment by brewing a pot of coffee using your tap water and then comparing it to a pot of coffee using bottled spring water. You could even borrow a pot of water from your friend's expensive whole-house water filtration system. Moreover, if you are serious about improving the taste of your water, you can seek the advice of the local coffeehouse in your area. Since they probably have the same basic water supply as you do, ask them if they filter their water or use bottled water.

Coffee Fanatic's Tip 16

Rather than invest in an expensive filtration system or buying bottled spring water first try an inexpensive small water filter – the kind the fits right over a pitcher that you can keep filled with cold water.

Coffee Fanatic's Tip 17

If your tap water is somewhat unpleasant but not that bad, use the same approach that I recommend for buying coffee (buy an everyday brand plus special occasion coffees), use cold tap water for everyday use and for those special occasions, use bottled spring water.

To sum-up about water:

Water is important – but do not become obsessive about it

- Cold water over hot water
- Filtered water over non-filtered water, if possible
- Bottled spring water may taste better than your tap water; then again, it may not.

3. Grinding the Coffee Beans

Once you grind your coffee, more of the total volume of grounds is now exposed to air so the coffee loses its flavor at a greatly accelerated rate compared to the larger, intact coffee beans. For this reason, it is best to brew your coffee immediately after grinding, certainly within the first hour.

Make sure that you grind to the right degree of coarseness depending upon the coffee and brewing method. For example, use a very fine grind for espresso, a coarse grind for coffee that you are planning to brew in a French Press, etc.

Coffee Fanatic's Tip 18

The extraction process of brewing water through the coffee grinds works best when the grounds are all the same size and as even as possible. There are two types of coffee grinders, one that uses a rotating blade, and a burr grinder that uses spinning metal wheels. The burr grinder although expensive does a better job in producing a more uniform grind thus giving you a more consistent and favorable cup.

Coffee Fanatic's Tip 19

Coffee grinders will retain the flavors and odors of previously ground coffees. So carefully clean them on a regular basis, making sure that you unplug the unit from the electric socket. Again, you may want to consider having one grinder for your every-day coffee and one for gourmet coffees that you brew on special occasions.

4. Measuring the Coffee

How large is a Cup?

When it comes to measuring things, everyone knows that a cup equals 8 ounces. That is, everyone except the Coffee Industry. They continue to give their brewing instructions based on an old fashion cup. They apparently believe that we are all drinking our coffee out of 6 Oz. tea cups when most of us use 8 Oz. + sized mugs. (When buying a cup of coffee at a coffeehouse or other location, the minimum size is usually 12 Ozs.)

How Many Cups does your Coffee Maker Hold?

Adding to the confusion is the fact that you cannot trust how many true 8-ounce size cups that your coffee maker holds. <u>There are no standards.</u> You will have to first measure the actual number of ounces that your coffee maker holds if you want to brew a good cup of coffee. Do not go by the pre-printed or etched numbers on the side of the coffee maker.

How Many Teaspoons or Tablespoons, or Scoops per Cup?

Sometimes there are just too many obstacles in the quest for a good cup of coffee. You will find directions for adding the correct amount of coffee per cup varying from "heaping teaspoons to level tablespoons, to scoops (often furnished by the coffee maker manufacturer). You will also find the instructions both in the coffee maker's guide and on the packages of coffee that you buy. Often the two sets of instructions conflict on the correct proportions of ground coffee to cups of water. Coffee experts are no help either as they like their coffee

Photo by Nadia Mercer

exceptionally strong. Some for example recommend adding 4 tablespoons per 8 Oz. cup while many commercial coffee roasters only recommend 2 tablespoons.

Trial & Error

The best approach is to find the right coffee/water ratio that suits your own taste preferences: Start by measuring the amount of water that your coffeemaker holds. Next start with a formula of two slightly rounded tablespoons for each 8 Oz. cup that you want to make. For example, if your coffee maker holds 32 Ozs. of water – 4 standard cups, try brewing 8 rounded tablespoons of coffee. Then make adjustments, increasing the tablespoons, leveling the tablespoons or reducing them until you find just the right formula for yourself.

Coffee Fanatic's Tip 20

<u>Brewing for more than one person</u>

Brew for the person that likes their coffee the strongest. Then dilute the coffee for the second person with hot water (your own version of an Americano). The Coffee will actually taste better (once you get the right amount of the coffee/hot water mix). Coffee will only taste bitterer if it is brewed at less than full strength and not be as favorable.

Brewing and Serving

As long as you pay attention to the selection, storage, and grinding of coffee beans as well as the importance of good water, the brewing and serving part is easy. Moreover, it can actually add to the ambiance of a special evening when friends visit. A long time friend of mine, Joseph Mattera who lives in Atlanta served one of the best cups of espresso that my wife and I have ever had. A few years ago, after dinning out at a nearby restaurant, we returned to his place for coffee. First, I was fascinated by the simple Neapolitan Flip pot that Joseph was using (see Chapter 5) to brew the espresso. Secondly, he did not use an expensive espresso specialty roast but instead, he used Medaglia d'Oro Espresso that can be found in most supermarkets. He served the espresso immediately after brewing. It was hot, bold and enormously favorable. He also served the espresso in plain but elegant white demitasse cups along with a dish of vanilla ice cream with plain biscotti on the side. The espresso was outstanding and the ice cream with biscotti was delicious! Before I forget, let me also add the astounding fact that the espresso was Decaf! Who says that Decaf cannot taste good and that you need expensive equipment to brew espresso?

The Power of Presentation

I relate the above story that happen in my personal life to illustrate two key essentials truths in brewing and serving coffee at home:

- A. You do not need an expensive coffee maker or gourmet coffee beans.
- B. The processing of brewing and serving coffee can be used to your advantage.

While I certainly encourage everyone to buy the best quality coffee that they can afford, especially for special occasions, you will find that not all your guests will appreciate it. Using the "Purchase Recommendations" chart in Chapter 4 as a guide, you may want to ask your local coffeehouse owner for a medium roast recommendation. Concerning the coffee makers, a few of them covered in Chapter 5 only cost in the $20.-$30. range from most of the suppliers that are listed under Coffee Equipment & Supplies in Section III. I do recommend that you have an alternative to your regular automatic drip model for special occasions.

Using the total brewing and serving process to your advantage, two coffee makers in particular offer you the opportunity to serve up a memorable cup of coffee that will definitely impress your friends: Both the French Press and the Vacuum Pot make excellent coffee. In addition, you can brew the coffee right on the table in front of your guests. Most of them will not have seen anyone use either brewing method in the past. As pointed out in the chapter on Coffee Makers, people may not remember the taste of the coffee that you served, but they will certainly remember how you brewed it. A few other items to enrich the brewing and serving process and to impress your guests are:

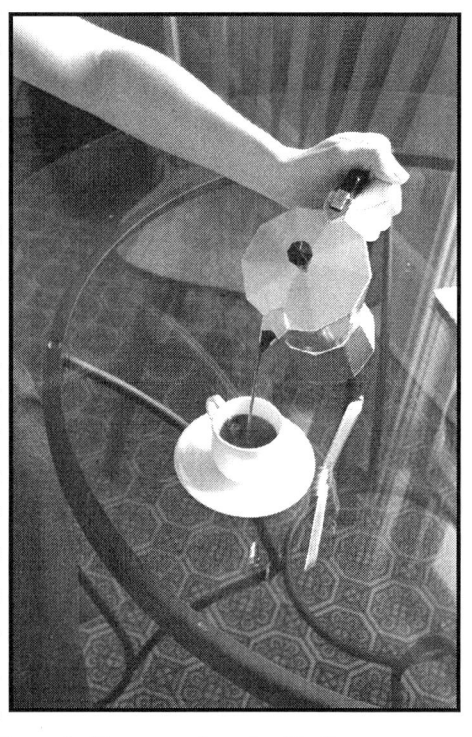

Photo by Nadia Mercer

The Cups

Do not underestimate the importance of the cup in leaving your quests in absolute awe of your coffee making abilities. First, always use the right sized cup. Straight espresso calls for an espresso-sized cup; usually a 3 oz cup. A Cappuccino requires a 6 oz cup. A latte for home serving should be appropriately served in a 10 oz cup.

Next, what the cup is made of is both important and it will add style to the presentation when you are serving coffee at home. Ceramic cups and mugs are among the best material for serving coffee in, as the flavor will not be corrupted. The white porcelain variety is also very elegant looking. In addition, both stainless steel and glass are excellent cups and provide the same benefits of not disturbing the flavor of the coffee nor retaining off odors from other drinks that may have been in them in the past. Both stainless steel and glass cups (they also come combined in one cup as the photo shows) should be in everyone's cupboard as they are highly stylish for entertaining one's guests. An additional quality of stainless steel cups is that they retain the heat of the coffee longer.

A 3 oz espresso cup made out of porcelain

Both Photos by Nadia Mercer

A 6 oz cappuccino cup made out of porcelain with a stainless steel base

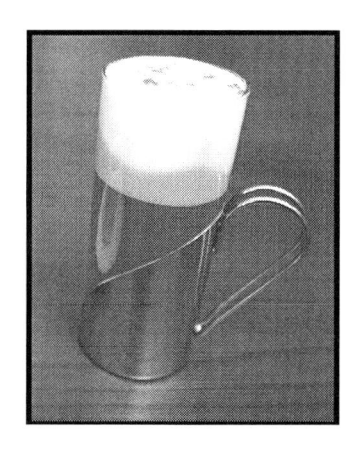

A 10 oz Latte cup made out of both stainless steel and glass

Photo by Nadia Mercer

Desert Pairings

Most purists believe that you should not serve anything with coffee. I disagree. Coffee is amazing in that it compliments and adds to the enjoyment of many foods and deserts. For deserts to serve with after-dinner coffee, here again your local coffeehouse is a great resource. They typically carry some of the best deserts and other foods that go well with coffee. And as an added bonus, items such as biscotti's and muffins are usually fresh and delicious as they are baked locally.

To give you some ideas, here are some of my favorite deserts that I have enjoyed over the years with coffee:

Brownies

Cakes, especially very rich tasting ones

Cheesecake, especially chocolate-toped ones

Chocolate covered almonds

Chocolate mousse

- Chocolate or mocha tarts
- Chocolate, plain - both white and dark
- Chocolate truffles
- Coffee cakes
- Cookies, especially chocolate chip, oatmeal raisins, and Oreos
- Danish rings
- Doughnuts
- Ice cream, preferably vanilla
- Ice cream cakes
- Italian pastries and cakes, especially biscotti, cannoli, almond tortes, napoleons, and sfugliatella
- Muffins, especially ones with chocolate or cappuccino chips
- Pie alamode
- Puddings
- Stollen
- Strudel
- Tiramisu
- Various pies, but especially blueberry

Of course, what you select should depend upon the occasion. If your coffee is being served after an informal lunch, doughnuts or Oreos might be appropriate. After a more formal dinner, vanilla ice cream and biscotti like those that my friend Joseph served certainly make for a more elegant compliment to your coffee or espresso.

Coffee Fanatic's Tip 21

Having some guests over for an informal lunch, serve a Yemen Mocha coffee with almond flavored Klondike Bars.

Coffee Fanatic's Tip 22

Don't know what to serve with espresso? Impress your friends by ordering a mixed biscotti tray from a true Italian bakery like Venieros in New York City. They have been in business since 1894 and offer various sizes of biscotti trays as well as other delicious pastries. (They can ship everywhere and you can reach them at www.venierospastry.com.)

Coffee Fanatic's Tip 23

When having someone over for afternoon or evening coffee, instead of coffee cake or other pastries, try serving some chocolate-covered coffee beans (some coffeehouses carry these).

Summary

In summary, the presentation of your coffee is just as important as the selection and brewing of the coffee beans. As long as you select good coffee and brew if fresh, you should have no problem serving a memorable cup. Concerning the freshness, the information from the chart from Chapter 4 on "Time Considerations ...." is also listed here to remind you how quickly coffee can loose its flavor.

Coffee loses its flavor:
- 2 Weeks After Beans Are Roasted
- 1 Hour After The Coffee Is Ground
- 15 Minutes After The Coffee Is Brewed

Postscript to Chapter 6

Here are some other helpful hints and "reminders" that you can do to serve a distinctive cup of coffee every time:

Putting It All Together – Helpful Hints

Plan your coffee brewing and serving in advance to avoid serving cool coffee or coffee that has lost its flavor.
Stir your coffee in the pot immediately after brewing to insure a more consistent taste for all your quests.
When serving a dark, almost black, coffee, use either a glass cup or a white porcelain one for a dramatic effect.
Coffeehouses frequently carry distinctive cups for purchase that will enhance the presentation of your coffee servings.
Always brew to the capacity of the coffee maker as it is engineered to brew correctly at that level.
Clean your coffee maker every other month by brewing a mix of 1 part vinegar and 4 parts water.
Warm your cups or mugs before pouring the coffee, as this will help keep the coffee hot longer.
After you fill your coffee maker with cold water, rinse out the carafe with hot water to keep the coffee hot longer.
Use a glass or stainless steel storage container as it is hard to get rid of odors in other types of canisters.
When making ice coffee in advance, store the brewed coffee in a covered container in the refrigerator.
When making ice coffee for immediate servings, brew using 1 ½ times the normal amount of coffee, which will offset the dilution from the ice that is added.

Chapter 7 – Exploring Other Coffee Habitats (Getting a Good Cup of Coffee on the Road)

Field Guide Chapter 7 Highlights

- *Coffee is being served everywhere across America*
- *Travel and have your coffee too*
- *Exploring everything from gas stations to fast food*
- *A sampling of what the hotels are doing*

What is a poor Coffee Fanatic to do when out traveling in search of a good cup of coffee? There is nothing more frustrating than being away from home and not being able to find a decent cup of java, much less a cappuccino or latte. For some of us it ranks right up there with life-changing events like moving, loss of job, divorce, etc. when we have to travel and can't find our favorite brew. Equally frustrating is when we find out that local or regional tastes and preferences can be a great deal different than what we are use to at our local coffeehouse.

Do I hear an "Amen" for Starbucks? For like HoJo's, Applebee's, McDonald's, and other large franchises there is a consistency of quality that one can expect in any of the Starbucks locations across the country. Pity the poor coffee connoisseur of 20 years ago who had no alternative but to drink overcooked, military-style, bitter coffee out of foam cups, commonly known as "rut-gut." Unfortunately Starbucks or other coffeehouse chains are still not everywhere. Especially as you venture out from our cities and suburbs to the more rural areas of America.

The Coffee Fanatic's guide would not be complete without looking at this total habitat where with a little ingenuity; we can get a good cup of coffee. Nothing is more disconcerting to a true coffee fanatic than to be away from our normal habit at the local coffeehouse and the friends that we can always count on to commensurate with about the daily trials and tribulations of life. It is also disconcerting to be away from that special bag of Kona or Costa Rican Tarrazu coffee that we are used to brewing at home in our French Press. But just like the thousands of animal and insect species in the rainforests, there are plenty of places in the overall American habitat where you can find a cup of coffee. To start, here is a partial list of some of the places that serve coffee across America:

The Greater Coffee Habitat
(Where you can try to get a good cup of coffee)
Airports
Art Galleries
Bagel shops
Bakeries
Bookstores
Bus Stations
Car Dealerships
College Campuses
Convenience Stores
Diners

Drive-Thru Coffee Stands
Fitness Centers
Fast Food Restaurants
Gas Stations
Hotels/Motels
Laundromats
Music Stores
Restaurants
Rest Stops
Shopping Malls
Sport Arenas
Supermarkets
Theaters
Train Stations
Truck Stops

Photo by Nadia Mercer

Coffee is being served everywhere these days. Many businesses have upgraded the coffee that they serve and even advertise about it. At some locations, like the hotel you may be staying in, it is even free (or hidden in the cost of the room rate). With all these locations available for us to find a first-rate cup of coffee, why is it so hard to do so when we travel outside of our normal habitat? Two basic reasons, one general and one very specific:

    1. The people in charge of the coffee do not realize the importance of each step in the brewing process.

2. Coffee at many of these places is often stale and lacking in flavor because it has been left in the pot too long.

While there is not much that coffee fanatics can do about these careless practices, here are some guidelines for travelers to avoid getting a sub-par cup. Let's face it, coffee is an important part of our lives and we deserve to have a quality cup at all times.

Coffee Fanatic's Tips for Finding a Good Cup on the Road:

Traveling By Car - Gas Station Coffee

The odds of getting a good cup of coffee at gas stations have increased dramatically over the past five years. Gas station companies like, BP, Chevron, Exxon, Shell, and Sheetz just to name a few, have both changed to better quality coffee roasts and now pay more attention to the preparation of coffee. Some of them are even serving espresso-based drinks. The Uni-Mart outlets, for example are now selling different roasts and flavored coffees from Green Mountain Coffee Roasters. Also, Seven-Eleven's and Dunkin Donuts (see recommendations later in this chapter) are frequently co-located with gas stations. In general, newer gas stations are planning bistro-looking surroundings for customers to both enjoy coffee plus meals. Naturally they recognize the importance of serving a top-notch cup of coffee.

Coffee Fanatic's Tip 24

Regardless of where you stop, here are three questions to always ask:

1. Is your coffee fresh?

2. What type of coffee do you use?
3. How long ago was it brewed? (Remember the 15 minute rule)

Coffee Fanatic's Tip 25

If you do see someone combining two pots to give the appearance of the coffee being freshly brewed, it is a sure indicator that the owner has no regard for coffee flavor or their coffee-drinking customers. Another good clue as to how serious the owner is about serving a good cup of coffee is if he or she commits that cardinal sin of using the same lids as those used for cold drinks - GET OUT OF THERE FAST!

Coffee Fanatic's Tip 26

Avoid Styrofoam cups like the Plague – Not only are they bad for the environment, this material can affect both the flavor and bitterness ("good" acidity) of the coffee. If you have no other nearby alternative, clean the cup with the hot water used for tea. This will not only sanitize the cup but it will remove any residue leftover from the manufacturing process.

There is a direct relationship between how clean the gas station looks and the quality of their coffee. There is also a correlation between how busy a gas station is and the quality of their coffee. This is probably mainly due to the fact that the coffee is constantly being purchased and therefore replenished than for any other reason.

Any gas station that has someone just assigned to the coffee station recognizes the importance of not serving stale coffee or having unclean brewing equipment. Another indicator of good coffee is the type of cups and lids that a gas station uses. Any station cutting corners here is probably also skimping on the quality of the coffee that they purchase plus the frequency that they dispose of stale coffee and brew a new batch.

Photo by Nadia Mercer

Look for a Cracker Barrel, Dunkin Donuts, MacDonald's, Seven-Eleven, etc.

First, Cracker Barrel's quality of coffee is a well kept secret. While the restaurant chain is well known to many travelers for their homestyle food and gift shop, not that many people know that you can get a consistently great cup of coffee at Cracker Barrel. Since they are all over the place, it is a stop that you can depend upon while traveling (currently, there are 560 locations in 41 states). Secondly, when I first starting writing this book, I would not even have thought of mentioning McDonald's. However, they have since embarked upon a campaign of serving a "**Richer, Bolder, and Taster Cup of Coffee**" and I can tell you that it is darn good. This is because they are using 100% Arabica beans plus, equally as important, they have trained their employees on the overall brewing process. In their March, 2007 issue, a leading consumer publication compared straight black coffees from Burger

King, Dunkin' Donuts, McDonald's, and Starbucks. They judged McDonald's to be the best of the four.

Dunkin Donuts, long an old time favorite with many Americans also turns out a constantly good cup of coffee in a variety of roasts. What is interesting to the automobile traveler is that there are more and more Dunkin Donuts that are co-located with gas stations. I know that when I travel, I would rather stop at a gas station that has a Dunkin Donuts than at one that does not.

Next on the list are Seven-Eleven stores. They started stocking better quality coffees in about 2005 and they offer a variety of roasts plus a self service station that allows the customer to choose different roasts, flavored coffees, flavored syrups, and various toppings.

Arriving In a Strange Town

If you are staying at a hotel, it will not hurt to call ahead to find out about their coffee. You may be surprised to find out that they offer first class coffee 24 hours a day. More hotels are doing this as they recognize the importance that Coffee Fanatics like us place on finding a good cup of coffee.

Upon arrival, inquire where they serve a good cup of coffee. Frequently, the hotel clerk will not be able to help you but you never can tell until you ask. You can always head to the nearest mall especially if it is late but not yet 10 p.m. Once there, you will probably find one or two of the more reputable franchises. An alternate to the Mall are some of the large chain Bookstores like Barnes & Noble, Boarders, & Books A Million. They are usually open until 10 pm and have either a Starbucks or a Joe Mugs coffee franchise in them.

If you are driving around town and it is still light enough out to see, be on the alert for where the old people are going out to eat. I do not mean that with any disrespect. Older people not only know where the good food is, and at a reasonable price, but they simply will not frequent a place that serves bad coffee. Older Coffee Fanatics, with the wisdom of their age, realize that no matter how good the meal is the price is not worth it if the restaurant serves a bad "Cup of Joe." Restaurants should realize that serving a good cup of coffee is simply good for business as the last thing people remember about their meal was the coffee that they were served.

When Eating In Restaurants

Like the food served by restaurants, coffee while dinning out can range from some of the best you have ever tasted to some of the worst. Complicating the Coffee Fanatic's life is the fact that there isn't always a direct correlation between the quality of the food and the quality of the coffee.

Photo by Nadia Mercer

A good sign is when the restaurant advertises or posts on their menu that they serve a certain type of coffee (100% Columbian for example). In addition, these days it is not considered impolite to ask, "What type of coffee do you serve?"

Coffee Fanatic's Tip 27
You can get freshly brewed coffee every time when dinning out. Just ask your server if the coffee is fresh. Inevitably this results in the server arranging for a fresh pot to be brewed for you.

A Sampling of Hotels

Below is a sampling of what hotels are doing in the area of serving better coffee. Many of them realize how important coffee is to us coffee fanatics. Some of them, in addition to improving there in-room coffees, have been setting up self-service coffee bars in their lobbies. In looking at this sampling, keep in mind that there are frequently regional differences in the type of coffee served based on the availability of certain suppliers and roasts. Plus different franchise arrangements and ownership obligations don't always require all locations within a large chain to serve the same type of coffee (Call ahead!).

<u>Hyatt</u> hotels is serving premium 100% Arabica coffee and making them more convenient for customers to get right at coffee carts in their lobbies.

<u>Hilton</u> hotels started in 2006 to equip some of their locations with in-room Cuisinart single brew coffeemakers along with

Lavazza dark roasted coffee. Some of the higher-end Hiltons have coffee carts with gourmet roasts in their lobbies.

Omni Hotels and Resorts started serving Starbucks coffee and espresso drinks in 2006.

Ritz-Carlton's serves gourmet coffees in their hotel restaurants and offers these coffees to their meeting room clients.

Sheraton is now serving Starbucks coffee in their corporate-owned hotels plus they have upgraded their brewing equipment.

Holiday Inn Express hotels now serve 100% Arabica coffee beans that they call "Smart Roast" with their free breakfasts.

Westin Hotels and Resorts are now offering in-room coffeemakers, featuring Starbucks coffees.

Coffee Fanatic's Tip 28

If you are not pleased with the vast improvements of coffee quality and brewing equipment when traveling, bring your own! It is not as preposterous as one might think. I would certainly recommend it if you are renting a condo for a few weeks. That remote paradise where the condo is located might not offer much of a gourmet coffee selection. But even for domestic trips, you can certainly pack your own coffee and frequently a small coffee maker. For driving, one coffee fanatic that I know uses a portable French Press and combined travel mug. It is stainless steel, insulated thermos made by Nissan. (See our list of coffee equipment suppliers in Section III, Recommended Resources, C.)

Chapter 8 – The Socially Responsible, Environmentally Friendly and Politically Correct Coffee Fanatic

Field Guide Chapter 8 Highlights
- *Gaining a prespective on a confusing situation*
- *Fair Trade, Organic, etc. - A dilemma for coffee lovers*
- *Reducing the "Greenhouse Effect"*
- *Have your coffee and donate too*

Are you a socially responsible coffee consumer?

Many of us think that we are. At least, in many areas of our life, we try. We do things like recycling, buying energy efficient products for our home, paying attention to where products are manufactured (and how the labor force is treated there), etc. In addition we are becoming increasingly aware of how each individual contributes to the ecology of the world. In short we want to be as "green" as possible. However, when it comes to purchasing coffee, there is a lot of confusing information being put on coffee bags these days.

For example, you just bought a bag of coffee and the little logo on the bag looks like this picture:

(The above depiction is the label of *TransFair USA*. For more information, visit their website:www.transfairusa.org)

You paid a little more for the coffee but you feel good about yourself for buying a fair-trade product. After all you did the right thing for the people who work on the coffee farms, the environment, etc. – or did you? Is your coffee bag for example, also stamped Bird Friendly, Certified USDA Organic, Shade Grown, approved by the Rainforest Alliance and does it support appropriate use and development of the land through the Sustainable Agriculture Network? If you bought your coffee at a coffeehouse or college shop, did it come in a biodegradable and compost-able cup with a recycled sleeve printed with soy ink?

No. Shame on you! If you did not buy a bag of coffee with all the above certifications stamped on it, can you truly call yourself a progressive citizen of the world and a protector of our eco-system? Also, in addition to the farmers getting a fair price and the environment of the coffee regions being protected, is part of the cost of your purchase being used to improve the education of the farmers' children, building better health care facilities, and financing alternate business opportunities in the seventy or so countries that coffee comes from?

Coffee Certifications

In theory to be the ultimate socially responsible coffee consumer, your coffee bag should have all the following logos stamped on it.

(The above depictions and logos, starting at the top and reading clockwise, are the labels of: *The Smithsonian Migratory Bird Center* - a division of the National Zoo, The *United States Department of Agriculture (USDA)* - Quality Certification Services, *TransFair USA, Catholic Relief Services - Nicaragua, The Rainforest Alliance* part of the Sustainable Agriculture Network (SAN) and *Catholic Relief Services* – For more information, see Section III, Recommended Resources for a listing of websites)

Ideally, there should also be a printed statement form the roasting company that reads something like this:

"We donate part of the profits from every bag of coffee to the *XYZ* charity."

Now, if you are Catholic, look for their special logo and stamp – CRS that stands for Catholic Relief Services. And if you are Jewish, in addition to all the above certifications and stamps, look for the K stamp indicating that you are getting coffee harvested under kosher conditions. In addition, is your coffee roasting company or coffeehouse a "green" business that focuses all phases of its operations on renewable energy and using recyclable material, etc.

MIND BOGGLING, ISN'T IT? Read on!

Frankly, no other commodity puts so many "guilt trips" on us consumers who are just searching for a good "cup of Joe". Plus by being bombarded with confusing labels and charitable statements, how is the average person to determine if they are first, buying a good bag of coffee and secondly, is the cause a just one. After all, in most cases you are paying a premium for these coffees.

With so many conflicting and competing certifications and corresponding definitions of what is correct, the resulting confusion over coffee harvesting, pricing, and consumption gives new definition to the term, "A Catch 22." For example, growing Certified USDA Organic coffee may have to be done in a controlled agricultural situation that may not offer the desirable rain forest canopy of tall trees above the coffee plants that would certify a coffee as, "Bird Friendly" or qualify the growing process as "sustainable agriculture" according to the Sustainable Agriculture Network. And what about situations that happen every year when small farmers face loosing their USDA certification or Fair Trade certification because they need to use insecticides to save their crop (and their income for that growing season) because of insect infestation? Nevertheless we all want to do our part to protect our global environment and to help assure fair wages and fair trade practices for all.

A Coffee Perspective

With all the current emphasis on being a conscientious global consumer in buying Fair Trade, in buying Organic, etc., it is important to understand how these issues came about and how they affect the coffee industry, worldwide.

1. Coffee has been part of a "Global Economy" long before the term was coined. First shipping in significant quantity from the Ports of Java and Mocha in Arabia to Europe in the early 1600's and then, as European colonization spread around the world, the South American crops were cultivated and were shipping to Europe and North America by 1800. From South America, to Africa, to Asia, the history of trading coffee has a colorful past laced with fierce competition. Coffee like oil and sugar is traded on international commodity exchanges with "futures" contracts being the trading vehicle that basically sets the wholesale price of coffee.

    Overall, and compared to other commodities, coffee being produced in about 70 countries, remains competitive and inexpensive in the worldwide market place. At times the coffee prices can drop ridiculously low like they did in 2000 forcing wide spread unemployment and increased poverty, especially in South and Central American countries. In countries like Honduras coffee is as much as 25% of their total exports so depressed coffee prices have a definite effect on their economy and the poverty level of their people. Unlike our friends in the Middle East who have become extremely rich off of our dependency on oil, the same is not true in proportionate numbers for our Latin American friends in coffee producing countries. To put this further in perspective, an average Mexican coffee farmer worker makes about $4.00 per day (US currency) but if he enters the US illegally, he will immediately start making $5. to $10. an hour. *Fair Trade* is a trading agreement used to circumvent this global market process, by establishing base prices with certain coffee growing cooperatives to assure that the coffee producers will always receive a base price regardless of the official wholesale price.

2. Coffee is frequently grown on farms that range from nothing more elaborate than a dozen coffee trees on a small piece of land in the mountains to coffee plantations of thousands of acres. While larger coffee plantations process the coffee cherries themselves, store them and deliver their green beans right to the port of export, getting close to final market price, small farmers have to deal with middlemen. The price that small farmers receive can be as much as 50% less than that received by the plantations.

3. The majority of Coffee, ever since it became a worldwide commodity, was organically grown in the shade, under larger trees. Exceptions of course existed in parts of Africa and Asia. The tall trees not only provide sun protection for the delicate coffee tree leaves and berries, but also provide nitrogen-rich topsoil which becomes the natural fertilizer for the coffee plants. In addition this canopy of taller trees furnishes an excellent habitat for birds and other animals. There was very little need for chemical fertilizers.

Starting in the early 1970's, hybrid varieties of coffee trees were developed that were lower in height (for easier picking) and could be grown in direct sunlight. By eliminating the forest around the coffee trees, more coffee could be planted per acre with greater plant yields and faster harvesting methods. In this search for higher crop yields and without any thought to the total biodiversity of the rainforests, millions of acres were guttered and replaced by open fields of coffee trees. In addition to the habitats of various plants, birds, insects, and other animals, water run-off and soil erosion were also impacted.

4. Coffee workers receive low wages picking the coffee berries on larger farms during the harvest. They are usually paid according to the amount picked. While labor conditions have improved greatly in certain countries of South and Central America (Costa Rica is a prime example) over recent years, these are still very poor people compared to our standards in America or in Europe.

5. Coffee has been grown around the world organically for centuries preceding World War II. It was during that time period that insecticides, including DDT were developed to kill insects that destroy fruit trees. Millions of dollars of crop damage in general are avoided annually through the use of insecticides and also, fungicides (chemical compounds) that control weeds and control the spread of Fungi. Many large coffee plantations started in the 1950's using various fertilizers and chemical sprays to both enhance the growth of their crops and to control insect infestation. As you might imagine, this can be an important aspect of coffee production especially in the rain forest habitats of the world. Many of the coffee plantation managers have been educated in

the use of insecticides and fungicides at the best agricultural universities of the world including those in the United States of America.

However, it is also true that numerous small farmers both in South America and in other parts of the world never have treated their coffee trees and surrounding plants and trees with any toxic chemicals. In many cases, they cannot afford them and in other cases, they simply are not available to them. Their crops and land are 100% organic. It is ironic now that they cannot sell their coffee as "Organic" without going through a lengthy process (3 years) and paying an expensive fee to become certified. Unfortunately many farmers cannot afford this certification process.

What about Quality?

With this background in mind and as we look through this coffee labeling and certifications maze, let us not forget the primarily reason for our purchase – to buy quality coffee at a fair price. And none of these labels, despite what you either assumed or were led to believe, attest to the quality of the coffee inside the bag. Adding to the confusion of sometimes seeing two or three different labels on the same bag is deciphering the statements from the various coffee companies (either on the bags or in their brochures). Many of them are cleverly written by their Public Relations' departments to give them the appearance of being extremely socially responsible.

What follows is a brief breakdown of these various certifications and charitable causes that you can match with your own values and interests in order to make an intelligent and quality coffee purchase in the future. As you will read, people's interests can be extensive. They can vary greatly and include: health concerns, helping assure the survival of the world's rainforests, helping people in developing third world countries, ending the US trade embargo against Cuba, the world-wide eco-system and protecting the habitats of birds and gorillas. The following explanations will help you in being a conscientious citizen in both buying coffee for home consumption as well as ordering your coffee drinks at your favorite coffeehouse.

FAIR TRADE CERTIFIED

Certifying group: *TransFair USA*, a chapter of the non-profit *Fair Trade Labeling Organization (FLO)*

Purpose: To give farmers a fair base price for their coffee crop - frequently 2-3 times more than they would have before they were organized into cooperatives.

Helps: Increase the standard of living of small coffee farmers and their families. The environment is also helped as annual inspections also focus on the total ecosystem of the coffee growing and harvesting.

Coffee Quality: The quality of most of these coffees is excellent because they come from the choice higher regions of South and Central America (Check www.coffeereviews for specific ratings).

Price: Prices are generally comparable to non-Fair Trade certified coffees.

Fair Trade certification means that a trading agreement has been established between the American coffee roasters and certain farming cooperatives. This agreement essentially circumvents the global market process, by establishing a set per-pound price with these cooperatives to assure that the coffee farmers will always receive a fair price regardless of the official wholesale price.

The Fair Trade Certified label means that your coffee has the approval of the TransFair USA chapter (a non-profit organization) of the Fair Trade Labeling Organization (FLO), an international association in over sixty countries. Inspections to assure certification are conducted annually. The FLO's primary focus is that the farmers who grow and harvest the coffee are paid a fair price for their labor. It is estimated that small coffee farmers in these fair trade cooperatives earn 3-4 times the amount for their coffee that they once earned as individual farmers. This is because they get a pre-set price regardless of the Market price when they sell their coffee. You may have noticed a variety of commodities and fruits and vegetables, especially from South and Central America, carry The Fair Trade Certified label. Interestingly, buying Fair Trade Certified coffee does not automatically mean that you will pay more for it than for other coffees. This is because coffee roasters deal directly with the farmers (in the form of a collectively owned Farming Cooperatives), eliminating the middlemen (known as coyotes) who frequently, in the past, took a large percentage of the in-country profits form coffee sales). In addition, the cooperatives offer other benefits to the farmers. For example, in many cooperatives, farmers are able to buy supplies & arrange for improvement loans at fair prices.

A Dilemma for Coffee Lovers

The Fair Trade Certification movement, which started in the Netherlands in the 1970's mainly through the efforts of Bert Beekman and Max Havalaar Quality Mark Coffee, has done a great deal to organize and improve the conditions of small coffee growers. However, by its very mission of ensuring fair prices to small family farmers, large and reputable coffee plantations are excluded from this Fair Trade Certification. Many of these large plantations grow some of the best coffee in the world and some also pay their employees a living wage for the country in which they are located. This presents a dilemma for those of us who want to be socially responsible and at the same time enjoy some of the best coffee available. After all if you are a wine aficionado, would you pass up a Bordeaux from Barons de Rothschild (Lafite) whose only crime is that it has been a long established large family business that has perfected the art of wine making? Of course not!

One needs to also be leery of slick brochures from large roasters and coffee companies that explain the virtues of Fair Trade and other types of certification. These coffee companies apparently see a marketing advantage in showing how committed they are to these causes. Interestingly even the large conglomerates like Kraft and Nescafe are coming out with Fair Trade coffee. Proctor and Gamble, for example, now offers both a Fair Trade Certificated coffee and a Rainforest Alliance Certified coffee through their Millstone division.

If you are in some of the New England States, you can now find Fair Trade Certified coffee at your local McDonald's. All of this activity in rallying around the flag of Fair Trade smacks as a major public relations move by all these companies. Unfortunately all of these marketing efforts and pronouncements may only serve to dilute the overall meaning of the Fair Trade movement regarding coffee. Whether a small coffee rooster, a major coffeehouse chain or a major coffee corporation, when you analyze what they are really saying, coupled with looking at their actual coffee products for sale, you will frequently only see a limited percentage of their total products labeled with Fair Trade rather than a total commitment to this cause.

ORGANIC

Summary:

Certifying group: The *United States Department of Agriculture (USDA) - Quality Certification Services (QCS).* Certification: is though an annual inspection.

Purpose: To assure that coffee is grown and processed without the use of pesticides or other toxic chemicals.

Helps: The overall eco system in which the coffee is grown and especially purifies the water supply in the local region that humans and animals drink.

Coffee Quality: While the taste of organics has improved over the years, in my opinion, they are not yet on par with some of the excellent coffees from around the world. One web site that you can visit for serious taste and various other quality recommendations on organic as well as regular coffee is www.coffeereview.com (See the List of Resources in the back of this book).

Price: The price of organic coffee, although coming down as more of it is harvested, will be slightly higher than regular coffee.

The USDA Organic label means that you are purchasing coffee that has been cultivated without using any toxic chemicals such as DDT or Malathion. Obtaining organic certification is a lengthy and costly process. Farmers must maintain actuate and detailed records. For anyone changing their operations to organic farming, it is a three-year process to ensure that the crop, the soil it grows in and the surrounding water supplies are truly chemically free. Organic coffee like other organically grown vegetables and fruit always cost more. Organic farming requires more attention and labor. Frequently, more coffee trees and corresponding land are required to yield the same size crop as non-organic coffee farms. Currently, most of the organic coffee comes from Southern Mexico and Peru. It is estimated that 85% of organic coffee is also Fair Trade Certified.

Health Benefits of Organic?

There are no health benefits in drinking organic coffee although there is no question that where organic coffee trees are grown, the eco-system is positively improved. With coffee, unlike most fruits and vegetables, the skin of the coffee berry and its pulp are first removed from the seed (the coffee bean) before the beans are shipped for roasting. The coffee beans are then roasted at approximately 400°F which will remove any possible chemical residues that could have gotten through to the bean. Then, of course, coffee beans after grinding are brewed at about 190°F. So unlike apples or pears where you are eating the other skin and pulp of the fruit, there is no danger of digesting pesticides or herbicides with the roasted and brewed coffee beans.

So, if you want to drink organic coffee, do so to improve the world's water supply, as this is where most of the toxic chemicals used as fertilizer and to treat plant disease winds up and also in the surrounding ground soil. And of course, us humans and animals are drinking the water and eating vegetables grown in the soil.

Other factors in considering organic coffee

In fairness to many coffee farmers around the world, many follow excellent farming methods and have not used pesticides or herbicides on their coffee crop (in some cases, they never can afford to use these chemicals). Yet for various reasons they don't incur the expense to become certified as organic. Here again, you will find your local coffeehouse owner very knowledgeable about the different coffees of the world and under what conditions they are grown.

A Word of Caution

The Organic label previously shown near the start of this chapter is the only official Organic label that lets you know that the producing farm of the coffee or any other product has been inspected and properly certified. Be alert to coffee companies that just state that their coffee is organically grown or who use either their own or another label from around the world indicating organic. It is not the same thing and these companies have not gone through the same rigorous inspections that bear the USDA certified Organic label.

While the taste of organics has improved over the years, in my opinion, they are not yet on par with some of the excellent coffees from around the world. One web site that can visit for serious taste and various other quality recommendations on organic as well as regular coffee is www.coffeereview.com (see the List of Resources in the back of this book).

BIRD FRIENDLY

Summary

Certifying group: *The Smithsonian Migratory Bird Center* (a division of the National Zoo)

Purpose: Gives certification to coffees grown under the umbrella of much larger trees as in rain forest habitats.

Helps: Various species of native and migratory songbirds such as warblers, hummingbirds, orioles, and grosbeaks. In addition, this certification also helps maintain the rain forests and their important eco-system

Coffee Quality: The quality of these coffees is usually excellent because they come from the choice higher regions of South and Central America (again, check www.coffeereviews for specific ratings)

Price: expect to pay about 5% to 10% more than a comparable non-certified specialty coffee

The "Bird Friendly®" logo means that you are purchasing coffee that has been grown under the canopy of Rain Forest trees, usually at high attitudes in South and Central American countries such as Brazil, Guatemala, Peru, & El Salvador. The certifying body, the Smithsonian Migratory Bird Center also assures that the farms granted certifications are also organic and of course, the coffee is shade-grown. The Smithsonian Migratory Bird Center, long concerned with the decrease of migratory bird habitats such as the South American Rain Forests, started this certification program back in 1997 and even though it only accounts for a small percentage of the coffee sold, it is steadily growing in popularity especially among bird lovers who are also coffee drinkers. In some rain forests the number of different bird species can exceed 175.

But you do not have to be a bird lover to appreciate the purpose of this certification program. Coffee trees grown in the rain forests of the world are normally of excellent quality and benefit the surrounding environment as well as being supported by it. While more efficiency in terms of coffee yield per acre can be achieved by destroying the rain forest and planting coffee trees in close rows, much of the plant and animal life suffer in the process including the habitats of migratory birds. In addition the rain forest with its huge hardwood trees, banana plants, and other fruit trees, provide a naturally organically balanced eco-system for fertilizing the soil and for providing natural predators to leaf eating insects that could destroy the coffee trees. Interestingly, in addition to the consumer paying a little more for this coffee, the coffee roasters pay the Smithsonian Migratory Bird Center $.25 for each pound sold.

RAINFOREST ALLIANCE CERTIFIED

Summary

Certifying group: *The Rainforest Alliance* which is the administrative arm of the Sustainable Agriculture Network (SAN)

Purpose: Like "Bird Friendly", Rainforest Alliance provides certification to coffees grown under the canopy of a variety of larger trees existing in rain forest habitats. Their certification however focuses on a combination of ecosystem factors as well as economic and welfare ones.

Helps: The emphasis of the Rainforest Alliance is on the total benefits of the rain forest eco-system plus the welfare of farmers and workers. This certification helps the overall environment, including soil quality, reduced erosion, and consequently, less dependency on chemical fertilizers and pesticides.

Coffee Quality: Usually excellent, again because like "Bird Friendly", the coffee comes from some of the best growing regions of Central and South America.

Price: expect to pay about 5% to 10% more than comparable non-certified specialty coffees

The Rainforest Alliance is the administrative arm of the Sustainable Agriculture Network and as such set and carry out the standards for certifying farms and their coffee crops as "Rainforest Alliance Certified." The Sustainable Agricultural Network consists of members worldwide including non-profit organizations in the leading coffee producing countries. When you purchase a bag of coffee with the Rainforest Alliance Certified label, you know that the coffee has been grown on farms that have been inspected at least once a year. These inspections are according to standards that include proper crop management, erosion controls, pollution controls, and the protection of wildlife. Rainforest Alliance certification also involves the protection of coffee workers assuring fair wages and safe working and sanity conditions.

SHADE GROWN

Summary

Certifying group: There is no certifying agency for Shade Grown coffee. Look for an indication on the bag that you are buying Shade Grown coffee. You can also talk to the local coffeehouse owner or check the roaster's website for a suitable statement that the coffee is Shade Grown. Of course, the "Bird Friendly" label or the "Rainforest Alliance" label automatically means that the coffee is Shade Grown.

Purpose: To support coffee growers that are helping to maintain the eco-system of the world's rainforests and their various habitats for birds, plants, and other animals.

Helps: Various species of native and migratory songbirds as well as the overall rainforests of the world which many believe to be critical to our survival as a planet.

Coffee Quality: The quality of these coffees varies. Many coffees that are shade-grown are among the best coffees of the world. However without an official certification program, you need to be cautious of this labeling as there are no inspections or guarantees backing up the Shade Grown statement.

Price: Generally, there is no price difference for the bulk of this coffee from general market prices. However, some of the estate grown coffees from some of the highest regions of South America, Jamaica (*Blue Mountain*), and Hawaii, (*Kona*) that are also shade grown are very expensive.

CRS FAIR TRADE

CRS stands for *Catholic Relief Services*, a charitable arm of the Roman Catholic Church. Having the CRS Fair Trade label means that the coffee has received the Catholic Relief Services stamp of approval. In examining the various certifications, while many of them are championing worthy causes like Bird Friendly or Shade Grown, CRS feels that the Fair Trade certification is the only certification that benefits the small farmer and his family in underdeveloped nations. Their seal is intended to further signal fellow Catholics and others that this is a coffee that will directly benefit the low-income people in these countries.

NICARAGUA FAIR TRADE

This is also a seal from *Catholic Relief Services* that indicates the coffee roaster is selling Fair Trade coffee grown in *Nicaragua*. *CRS* is highlighting Nicaraguan Coffee because of the extreme poor living conditions there. While coffee harvesting started in the late 19th. Century, Nicaragua and coffee have been a tumultuous combination, not to mention the other problems the country has had with its dictators, inflamed politics and natural disasters like the leaf infestation of the mid 1970's. And who will soon forget the bloody revolution against the Somoza dictatorship in the 1980's, led by the Sandinistas, which left tens of thousands dead and close to a million Nicaraguans homeless.

Coffee farmers who did not agree with the Sandinistas had their farms appropriated even though many of them initially supported the revolution. Large coffee plantations were confiscated outright and taken over by the Sandinistas. Many of the coffee cooperatives formed by the government at that time were communistic in nature. The formation of the Contras and the ensuing battles against the Sandinistas has basically left Nicaragua in the state that is in today, an extremely poor country with sub-standard living conditions (especially among the small coffee farmers and workers). At one point, the United States who many of you will recall backed the Contras in the counter-revolution put an embargo on products from Nicaragua*.

Today, of course, there are no restrictions on purchasing coffee from Nicaragua. Catholic Relief Services is placing special emphasis on helping the farmers and their families by placing the special Nicaraguan label on coffee from that country. The Nicaraguan label also carries the Fair Trade label.

* "Uncommon Grounds," by Mark Pendergrast listed under Books in Section III - **Resources** gives a good explanation of this period in Central America's history and how the coffee industry was negativity impacted – not only in Nicaragua, but also in El Salvador, Guatemala, & Honduras.

How can Coffee Fanatics Reduce the "Greenhouse Effect"?

Being aware of the direct and indirect effects of our individual coffee consumption can help to reduce the demand for fossils fuels. It is fossil fuels used in the generation of energy such as coal, gasoline and natural gas that increase the level of carbon dioxide in the atmosphere creating the "Greenhouse Effect" which increases global warming. Since many of us drink a lot of coffee and coffee drinks, the sum total of our individual efforts in making responsible choices could be quite significant. Here are some things that we all can do:

•Invest in a coffeemaker with a thermal carafe. You will use less electricity compared with a hotplate type that continues to draw current after the coffee is brewed.

•Reduce both waste and energy used in manufacturing paper filters by using a metal mesh coffee filter.

•Do not throw out coffee grinds but use them as compost or a direct fertilizer for your plants or garden.

•Bring your own mug to the coffee shop, reducing the need for paper or foam cups. Most coffeehouses encourage this practice.

•If you use bottled water at home, switch to the large size, reusable bottled water service, if possible.

•Remove the "tie-down" strips from empty coffee bags and use them around the house as twists.

HAVE YOUR COFFEE AND DONATE TOO!

As mentioned at the start of this chapter, some of the coffee that you shell out $10. or $12. to buy will also mention on the bag certain charities that part of your purchase price (and frequently part of the roaster's profits) will go towards a specific charity. Why not? Bill and Linda Gates and Angelina Joliet can't do it all by themselves.

If you read some of the books listed in the Section III - **Resources** section you will find that there is a diverse and interesting group of entrepreneurs who got into the coffee business for various reasons. Unlike other business people, some of them did not start Coffee Companies with strictly a profit motive in mind. Many owners are very altruistic and sincerely concerned about the plight of the coffee farmers and coffee workers around the world. They are also frequently concerned about the environmental impact of bringing coffee to the marketplace. Some however tend to act in ways that draw attention to themselves rather than to their cause. One gets the impression by reading some of their escapades that they are running around the coffee growing regions of South and Central America plus Africa as either a stereotypical "Ugly American" or the comical Dortmunder in a Donald Westlake novel.

While in the process of pursing their activities to do what they perceive as beneficial for the coffee growers, they sometimes oppose the policies of local governments, international coffee regulating agencies, and even our own United States Government. There our however many worthy courses related to the plight of the coffee growers, pickers, and their families. While it seems like every coffee roaster has a favorite charity, some of the noteworthy ones that you may want to participate in through your own coffee purchases or even through a direct donation are:

1. Boca Java

Boca Java, a Florida-based coffee roaster has established a program to support our American Military. This program started out in 2003 as "Operation Million Cup" with the goal of sending a million cups of coffee to our troops overseas. With that goal already having been achieved, Boca Java's current program is now called, "Operation 2 Million Cup." They both discount the coffee in this program and match their customer's contribution. The program is extremely flexible in that, among other things, one can designate a specific military troop address in Iraq, Afghanistan, or Kuwait that you would like the coffee sent to. Their website is www.bocajava.com

2. Café Femenino

This program helps to market the coffees grown by over 400 women in Peru. Their coffees are both Certified Organic and Fair Trade Certified. In buying Café Femenino Coffee, you are contributing to the welfare of these women coffee farmers and their families. Frequently these families consist only of the woman and their children. The Café Femenino foundation markets their coffees to various coffee companies and coffeehouses in the United States. The foundation helps these women coffee farmers in a variety of ways from health care to improved roads in the communities that they live in. Typically, a percentage of the coffee bag sale will go back to the charity. These donations vary anywhere from $.01 to $.25 per bag purchased. You can also make a direct donation to Café Femenino through Pay Pal. Their website is www.cafefemeninofoundation.org.

3. Coffee Corps

The Coffee Corps was established as a joint volunteer program of the United States Agency for International Development and The Coffee Quality Institute in 2003. It encourages people who are professionals in the coffee field to join and contribute their skills to aid the coffee farmers of the world. You can participate by either making a direct donation, buying the coffee labeled "Q" Coffee (2% of the coffee auction proceeds go to local community projects) or by volunteering if you believe that you have the skills to contribute. They are currently operating in El Salvador, Guatemala, Nicaragua, Panama, Kenya, Columbia, and Zambia. The Coffee Quality Institute's website is www.coffeeinstitute.org.

4. Coffee Kids

Coffee Kids was founded by American coffee roaster Bill Fishbein in 1988. Their mission is to improve the lives of children and families in the coffee growing regions of the world. They develop specific programs that help the local communities become self-sustaining. Their activities span helping the local families start businesses (non-coffee related) to developing educational programs for the children. They are currently running programs in Nicaragua, Costa Rica, Mexico, and Guatemala. They raise money both through direct donations as well as through coffee retailers donating part of the profit from the sale of a specific blend(s) – this is when you will see them mentioned on the side of a bag that you may be considering for purchase. Their website is *www.coffeekids.org*.

5. Pura Vida Coffee

Pura Vida coffee was co-founded by Chris Dearnley and John Sage in the late 1990's. They are a coffee roasting and coffee supply business that is also an impressive charity devoted to helping the people in the coffee growing regions of the world. While having a business and a charity in the same organization seems to be an oxymoron, they apparently have pioneered this type of business that can compete vigorously in the marketplace yet use their profits for charitable efforts. They only purchase 100% Fair Trade

Certified coffee that in itself is unique in the coffee business. (Only 3.7% of Starbucks purchases for example, in 2005 were Fair Trade.) Selling a lot of their coffee through colleges and universities, they also sponsor Spring Break and other tours of coffee regions to raise awareness for their cause. One major existing program focuses on at-risk children in Costa Rica. You can contribute to their causes by both buying their coffees and through direct donation. Their web site is www.puravidacoffee.com

6. Thanksgiving Coffee

Thanksgiving Coffee is a Specialty Coffee Roasting company that is been in business for over thirty years. Their owners, Joan and Paul Katzeff are deeply involved with improving the lot of the coffee workers and the environment, world-wide as well as with some other causes such as the plight of mountain gorillas in Rwanda and ending the US embargo against Cuba. One participates in their causes through the purchase of the specific coffees aimed at a particular charity. They also have a joint venture between their company and The American Birding Association in which $.15 of every bag purchased of their *Song Bird Coffee* is donated to the association. Their website is www.thanksgivingcoffee.com.

7. Daily Grind

Daily Grind is a chain of coffeehouses that started in Virginia but is now nation-wide. Started in the 1990's, they now have over 65 coffeehouses and growing. They have a partnership with Project Hope, the international health organization that operated the S.S. Hope, a hospital ship that furnished health services worldwide, during the 1960's. They currently provide medical training, supplies and health care education. Their projects vary from offering health care in Nicaragua and Guatemala to offering health training to the communities affected by the 2004 Tsunami in Indonesia.

To support this worthy cause, Daily Grind developed a special blend of coffees called "Plantation Blend" which combines the finest coffee beans from Guatemala and Nicaragua plus coffee beans from Indonesia. $4.00 from every bag purchased goes to Project Hope. What is also unique about this partnership, if you would like to make a direct donation, Daily Grind will facilitate it and you can even specify if you want your funds to go to Guatemala, Nicaragua, or Indonesia – or to the overall Project Hope charity. Their website is www.dailygrindunwind.com

Misc. Labels & Socially Responsible Coffee Companies

There really seems to be no limit to the logos, certifications and the type of causes that you will see on the label of bags of coffee that you may purchase. While some of the main ones were mentioned above, here are some others that you may come across:

ISO 9000 and ISO 14000

When you see this on a bag of coffee it means that the coffee beans were grown, harvested, and processed according to a set of international quality standards. These standards, agreed to by over 157 countries, insure among other things, that the supply of services and commodities will be more efficient, safer, and cleaner. This ISO labeling indicates that the coffee growers, processors, and roasters have met international standards for the coffee industry. The ISO 9000 labeling attests to the quality of the overall coffee growing and harvesting operation while the ISO 14000 refers to the treatment of the overall habitat where the coffee is grown.

The Cooperative Coffees label

This label only serves to further bewilder the consumer as it merely signifies an importer for American and Canadian coffee companies who are members of this cooperative. While they import Fair Trade and organic coffee for over 20 coffee roasters, the Cooperative Coffees label is not a certification so it does not replace the Fair Trade or USDA Organic labels. Why this label is on the bags of some member companies is, in my opinion, confusing for the consumer?

Fair Trade, Organic Plus a Total "Green Business"

One coffee company that I am aware of does it all, **Grounds for Change** – they do it all when it comes to supporting the coffee growers, being concerning for the world's eco-system, and operating their business in such a way to minimize their utilization of the earth's ital resources. They are above all a Green Business which means that they "minimize waste, recycle, and focus much of their work in life-supporting products and services – affordable housing, sustainable agriculture, education, clean energy and efficiency, fair trade, pollution control, and community health care."*

Among the various activities that Grounds for Change are involved with are:

> They carry 100% certified Fair Trade, organic certified and shade grown coffees.

> They contribute 2% of their sales to the "1% for the Planet" organization.

*(Co-op America Business Network, *"What's a Green Business?"*
- from the home page of the Co-op Business Network, the Internet
- world-wide web, 7/21/06.
http://www.coopamerica.org/cabn/about/whatis.cfm)

They are a corporate member of "Coffee Kids"

They pay a premium to buy 100% renewable energy from their power company. This allows the power company to replenish the energy that Grounds for Change uses with sustainable wind, solar, or biomass energy.

They use 100% re-cycled paper.

They are endorsed by Catholic Relief Services, recognized by the Songbird Foundation, and are members of the Fair Trade Federation, Transfair of America, Co-op America, and The Northwest Shade Coffee Campaign.

They also sell Café Femenio Coffee (mentioned above) and donate $.25 of each bag sold to the Café Femenino Foundation.

Conclusion

So with this plethora of charities and worthwhile causes, what can the average Coffee Fanatic do? Should we concentrate on quality and let the global economy eventually sort things out. Or do we indeed have an obligation to help the people responsible for bringing us our pleasurable morning coffees, lattes, etc? And what about this planet earth that we all live on?

To start, it is helpful to keep in mind the legitimate certifications and charities and separate them from the marketing hype that we are frequently subjected to. I trust that this chapter is helpful to this end. One also needs to be alert to clever terms that imply certification but are not - like "grown under sustainable conditions" and "organically harvested".

In buying Fair Trade, we are indeed making a charitable contribution to the coffee growers and their families since they are receiving a premium over the market price. (At the time of publication of this book the market price of coffee, although fluctuating daily, is about $.90 per pound compared to the $1.26 guaranteed to Fair Trade cooperatives. The individual farmers do not necessarily get the whole $1.26 as some cooperatives deduct for their services and overhead. While economists that believe a free and open global marketplace coupled with crop yields and quality should ultimately drive the price of coffee, the Fair Trade program certainly helps to solve short term conditions in the poorer coffee regions of the world.

Is Fair Trade and even Organic Certification just however, to all the coffee growers and coffee regions of the world since many are excluded or don't choose to join coffee growing cooperatives? Some small independent coffee growers can not even afford the cost of certification. It should also be noted that none of the various industry coffee associations, either in the United States or world-wide can agree on supporting Fair Trade labeling, other labeling, or a common labeling and certification system that would make things a lot easier for consumers. One need only look at the 2004 Fair Trade Position Statement of the Specialty Coffee Association of America (SCAA) which has been posted on their web site. While appearing to commit to Fair Trade Certification, the position statement goes on to state that Fair Trade is "one effective way...." Their closing paragraph says it all, "SCAA also recognizes that there are other ways for members to promote the concepts of equitable trade, sustainability and transparency. We encourage all members to source their coffees in ways that support these ideals."

Buying Charitable Donation Coffees

Purchasing coffee that you enjoy that also donates part of their profits to a specific charity is certainly easier and less confusing than the mystification that surrounds the certification labeling process. There are many more charities than the few listed above. Some coffee roasting companies donate to world-wide causes while some concentrate on helping to satisfy needs within the United States. And if these companies are also environmentally active and support some of our concerns, like protecting the songbirds' habitats, so much the better! As mentioned elsewhere in this book, your local coffeehouse owner is an invaluable source of relating this labeling information to the quality of the coffees that you may be interested in.

Photo by Nadia Mercer

Coffee is the common man's gold and like gold, it brings to every person the feeling of luxury and nobility. (Sheik Abd-al-kadir)

Strong Coffee, much strong coffee is what awakens me. Coffee gives me warmth, waking an unusual force and a pain that is not without very great pleasure.

(Napoleon Bonaparte)

Chapter 9 – Health Taxonomy & Calories

Field Guide Chapter 9 Highlights

- *Why coffee is the new health food*
- *Then and now – myths vs. truths*
- *Understanding the disadvantages of coffee*
- *Enjoy your favorite coffee drink and loose weight*

Medical Disclaimer: *The author in not a health expert and in no way seeks to convey medical advice in this chapter or for that matter, in this overall field guide. As with all things concerning individual health, professional medical advice should be sought.*

Is Coffee Good For You or Bad for You?

Because of the popularity of coffee over the years, it has been and continues to be the most studied drink that we humans consume. Coffee's reputation has been a roller coaster of highs and lows concerning its health benefits ever since 525 AD. As mentioned in Chapter 1, it initially was consumed for medicinal purposes. Although caffeine was discovered in coffee back in the 1800's, in modern times (the last 50-75 years) the drug has been attributed to a number of diseases from cancer to heart problems. Many people, over the last 35 years switched either fully or partly to Decaffeinated because they were concerned about some of the reported implications of coffee but yet, did not want to give up their favorite drink. In 1969, the National Coffee

Association was so concerned about unsubstantiated studies, they established a Scientific Advisory Group to conduct their own research on the positive or negative aspects of coffee and caffeine.

Fortunately, today with the help of more sophisticated studies and advanced research techniques, practically all of the earlier claims have been disputed. In fact most of the earlier studies were "association" studies and not "causation" studies. In other words, a study would factually report that a certain percentage of factory workers had heart disease and since most of them drank coffee, coffee became one of the culprits by association. Presently, to the surprise of most Coffee Fanatics, it turns out that coffee is actually good for our health. The benefits of drinking coffee were even exulted in the August 2006 Fitness Magazine[1] as one of the top 10 things you can do to improve your health and live longer.

Why Is Coffee the New Health Food?

The main reason for coffee's reincarnation as a health food, in addition to new studies clarifying the effects of caffeine, is the emergence of the value of antioxidants over the last decade. And coffee is loaded with beneficial antioxidants.

Antioxidants can help reverse the tissue damage caused by the negative effects of oxygen on the body. This tissue damage contributes to aging, and to diseases associated with the aging process. In addition, coffee provides chlorogenic acids that reduce glucose concentrations[2].

Coffee is definitely a stimulant that raises metabolism, boosts blood sugar and consequently prevents fatigue.

Note: *See the end of the chapter for all the footnote explanations*

The caffeine drug in coffee also stimulates the nervous system. Coffee overall increases metabolism, and fuels the nervous system.

Other recent benefits include the capacity of coffee to fight depression, help to increase your memory, boost your ability to learn, improve human performance and contribute to fluid balance in the body.

Coffee and Health
Past Beliefs vs. Present Evidence

	Then	Now
Heart Disease	1960's studies implicated coffee in causing heart disease. Also a similar conclusion was made in a 1972-1973 Boston University study.	Both the American Medical Association and the British Heart Foundation concluded separately in 1996 that coffee does not contribute to heart disease or stroke[3]. A study in Scotland showed that coffee drinkers had a lower rate of heart disease[3]. Another study in Spain in 2006 showed that those who drink six or more cups a day have less heart disease risk that those people who drink one cup or less daily[4].

	Then	Now
Cancer, colon	In 1971, a Harvard researcher linked coffee to bladder cancer.	Current studies do not indicate such a link. As mentioned at the start of this chapter, coffee's antioxidants help to fight the formation of cancer cells in the body. In fact, a 2004 German study identified Methylpyridunium, an antioxidant that boosts blood enzymes helping to protect against colon cancer[5].
Cancer, liver	In the 1960's, coffee was believed to have caused liver cancer.	One recent study reported that the risk of getting liver cirrhosis is reduced by as much as 80% in people who drink coffee regularly[6].
Parkinson's	Ever since Parkinson's disease was identified there have been some who have suspected coffee as the culprit.	More than 5 separate studies have linked the reduction of Parkinson's Disease in people who drink coffee on a regular basis. These studies indicate that men, especially benefit in disease avoidance by drinking coffee[7].

	Then	Now
Gallstones	Dating back to the 1930's, people though that drinking coffee contributed to a build up of gallstones.	The risk of getting gallstones was decreased by 40% in men who drink two to three cups of coffee per day, according to a 1999 study published in the American Medical Association Journal[8].
Type II Diabetes	Research did not turn up any past studies linking coffee to Type II diabetes	Recent international studies as well as one published by the Journal of the American Medical Association have indicated that the risk of contracting Type II diabetes is reduced in coffee drinkers and directly proportional to the amount that you drink daily[9].
Other Possible Health Benefits Although less conclusive than the studies above, it has been suggested by various sources that the ailments on the right can be reduced or helped in being prevented with the consumption of coffee.		• Alzheimer's • Breast Cancer • Kidney Stones • Headaches • Symptoms of asthma • Loss of memory in elderly people

Performance/Safety Benefits	
There is no question that coffee's power as a stimulant contributes to improved performance and safety. Productivity is better and there is typically increased alertness and resulting improvements in creativity for both professional and artistic endeavors from drinking coffee. On the right is a summary of these benefits.	• Keeps drivers alert • Heightens learning • Increases endurance • Elevates energy levels • Keeps workers alert on night shifts • Improves athletes' results
Old Myths	
There have always been a lot of myths about coffee dating back to its early history. Some examples of these myths that are not true are on the right.	• Coffee impedes growth in young people • Drinking coffee will result in dehydration • Coffee causes leprosy

So, what are the disadvantages of Coffee?

Nowadays there is not much being published in a negative way about coffee. Below however is a summary of the key disadvantages:

1. Excessive caffeine affects the release of gastric acid in people causing a sour stomach in some. Conversely coffee helps other people's digestive system.

2. While the caffeine from normal coffee consumption (4-5 cups per day) will not harm most people, excessive consumption can cause nervousness and cause some people to have difficulty getting asleep. In addition since caffeine is a diuretic, the increased

production of urine can pose problems in people with urinary problems[10].

3. Pregnant women should probably not drink more than two cups a day because of possible risks associated with caffeine to the unborn[11]. **Important Note:** One's doctor should be consulted about any liquids to be consumed during pregnancy including coffee.

Important note about caffeine

For caffeine to be truly deadly to your body, one would have to drink about 100 cups all at once. However, excessive coffee drinking, e.g., about 10 cups in a row, could cause "vomiting, fever, chills, and mental confusion"[12].

Important note about coffee studies

Practically all of the past studies have been about typical cups of coffees (black or with a small amount of milk and sugar) and normal size cups (typically 6oz.). Certainly future studies will have to be done on people drinking American-sized coffee drinks such as Grande Lattes (16 Oz.), Café Mochas, various iced coffees, etc.

Additional Benefits – Health & Otherwise

Coffee vs. Green Tea

According to a study conducted by the Nestle Research Center in Switzerland, coffee has four times the antioxidant content as green tea and also more than red wine and cocoa.[13]

Sell yourself, your products, and influence others;
All over a "cup of Joe"

An Australian study[14] has shown that people are more apt to listen to and be persuaded by your point of view after sitting down together and enjoying a cup of coffee. Part of the reason for this is that coffee increases a person's ability to concentrate, making them better listeners. Coffee also puts people in a better mood thus making them more agreeable and open to your ideas.

Coffee Fanatic's Tip 29 on coffee studies and health

As future studies are released, and they will be, pay attention to who funded the research. This is often, but not always, an indicator as to whether there was an ulterior motive behind the study. Also examine inquisitively how the study was conducted. If you do have concerns about your own coffee consumption, seek the advice of a medical professional.

Coffee and Calories

Note: The calories listed in this section have been determined, for the most part, from information available through the United States Department of Agriculture. A few calorie counts have been taken from company websites. You have to realize that the calories in coffee drinks will vary from coffeehouse to coffeehouse depending upon how they make their drinks and the suppliers that they use for different ingredients. Even within large coffeehouse chains, the caloric content will tend to vary by location according to the individual employees making the drinks. <u>Remember, it is always best to check with the local coffeehouse owner.</u>

At the start of this chapter, one of our highlights states ***"Enjoy your favorite coffee drink and loose weight."*** At the risk of appearing foolhardy, I do think that is possible to significantly contribute to your weight loss goals through making minor changes to your favorite coffee drink. Of course if you just drink black coffee, you might as well skip this segment as an 8 ounce cup of coffee has about 2 calories. Drinking 8 cups a day, will boost your total daily calories from coffee to a gigantic 16.

Why Count Only Calories?

Most coffee drinks have nutritional value in that they contain carbohydrates, different types of fats, protein, and sugar. With apologies to all the popular diets, keeping track of calories, that are really a measurement that quantifies energy, are important to controlling or loosing weight. Considering just our example below of modifying a Grande hazelnut latte, you can save 240 calories a day. On a seven day basis with everything else being equal, the total of 1680 calories equates to a ½ pound weight loss each week! Simply put, if you consume more calories than your body needs or can burn as energy, you will gain weight. Consume less and you will loose weight.

More of us Coffee Fanatics are drinking a variety of coffee drinks including lattes, café mochas and iced coffee drinks in the Summer such as Frappuccinos,® Coffee Coolatas,® and other similar drinks served at our favorite coffeehouses. The number of calories from coffee drinks can vary anywhere from 100 to over 700 depending upon the ingredients and of course the size drink that you order. Since it requires either burning or reducing calories by 3,500 to loose 1 pound, controlling your intake of them can contribute to weight loss. Of course, the dilemma is how to do this while continuing to enjoy quality coffee drinks.

One advantage of counting coffee drink calories is that almost every coffeehouse owner can inform you about the calories in their drinks plus they can suggest different alternatives such as skim and soy milk. Some coffeehouses even have all the calories of their various drinks either posted or available for the asking as a handy reference. There is also a general chart in this chapter to help in understanding calories in coffee drinks. While it may be difficult to estimate the calories in a restaurant meal, you can pinpoint precisely how much your daily latte(s) are adding to your diet.

Let us start by understanding the calories that you are getting from your current coffee drink and the combination of ingredients in it. The first list illustrates the range of calories coffee drinkers are consuming based on some of the more popular drinks:

4 ¾ calories	Cup of black coffee (8 Oz.)
15 calories	Espresso W 1 tsp of sugar (1 ½ Oz.)
65 calories	Cup of coffee W cream & sugar (8 Oz.)
130 calories	Cappuccino - whole milk (12 Oz.)
260 calories	Latte - whole milk, no flavoring (16 Oz.)
300 calories	Mocha – whole milk (16Oz.)
350 calories	Coffee Coolata® – whole milk (16Oz.)
470 calories	Frappuccino® W whip cream (16Oz.)
570 calories	Mocha Moolatte® W whip cream (16Oz.)

Add a flavoring to your latte and you will tack on another 80 calories. Do you like whip cream with your coffee drinks? Depending upon who is making it, figure on another 100 - 150 calories. Conversely, you can reduce the calories you are getting from your daily self-indulgence by changing from whole milk to low-fat or by switching from sugar to a sugar substitute. There are so many options open to you that coffee drinks (unless you are just having a "cup of Joe" black) indeed offer significant opportunities to control or loose weight. Some of these changes however do involving acquiring a taste for some of the drink substitutes. Surprisingly however, many people do switch their ingredients and adapt to the new taste rather quickly. Do not forget considering the obvious step (with no taste difference at all) – scale down from your current 16 Oz. drink to a 12 Oz. drink. You can save 55 calories if you drink cappuccinos or 65 calories if you switch to a 12 Oz. latte.

This next chart displays the difference changing your milk type and ingredients can make:

CALORIES	Differences In Milk			When You Add Ingredients			
	Whole Milk	2% Milk	Skim Milk	Flavor Syrup	Whip Cream	1 Tsp Sugar	1 Tsp Garnish*
Regular Coffee	25	21	18	—	—	+ 15	+ 10
Cappuccino 12 Oz.	130	90	50	+ 80	+ 100	+ 15	+ 10
Latte 16 Oz.	260	220	160	+ 80	+ 100	+ 15	+ 10
Mocha 16 Oz.	300	260	220	+ 80	+ 100	+ 15	+ 10
*Avg. for 1 Tsp (Cinnamon = 6 calories, Nutmeg = 12 & Chocolate shavings = 15)						

As you can see, a coffee drink, depending upon your likes and preferences, can really add up to a meal in itself. The good news is that unlike so many other food and drink types, there are a lot of options for changes and substitutes to reduce your caloric intake. For example, if you normally drink a Grande (260 Calories) hazelnut (80) latte with two sugars (30), whip cream (100), and a chocolate shavings topping (15) – <u>you are really drinking a whopping 485 calories.</u>

Photo by Nadia Mercer

(And hopefully you are only having one of these a day.) Alternatively, if you change your order to a Grande skinny (skim milk – 160) Whipless (0) hazelnut (80) with two "Cher" sugars (0), - you will cut your calories in half, drinking just 240 calories. Plus, except for the absence of whip cream and chocolate topping, you are essentially having the same drink.

And once you get used to this drink, switch from regular hazelnut syrup to "sugar free" hazelnut syrup for an additional 80 calories savings. <u>An overall 67% reduction in calories!</u> Incidentally if you do not want to give up the whip cream, ask for half the normal amount. Plus many coffeehouses have "light" or "Low Cal" whip cream but you have to ask for it.

Coffee Fanatic's Tip 30

To close this chapter, here are some tips for considering calories in both making and serving coffee drinks at home:

1. *Serve your cold coffee drinks in 12 Oz. or smaller glasses. If you do use larger glasses, use plenty of ice. Also, consider getting some of the more elegant tall but narrow glasses*

2. *Have both sugar substitutes and sugar free syrups on hand to give you guests options*

3. *Buy the ready whipped, "light" cream*

4. *Your guests will never know the difference if you switch from whole milk to low fat milk. For your own daily drinks, acquire a taste for coffee drinks made with skim milk.*

5. *In the summertime plain ice coffee is a refreshing everyday drink. With low fat milk and a sugar substitute added, a 12 Oz. drink is only going to run about 20 calories. (Remember to brew the coffee and refrigerate it ahead of time to minimize the amount of ice needed thus keeping your drink at full strength.*

Chapter 9 Footnotes

Footnote 1: "10 Reasons You're Healthier Than You Think" <u>Fitness Magazine</u> August 2006 80+
Footnote 2: Bakalar, Nicholas. "Coffee as a Health Drink? Studies Find Some Benefits" <u>New York Times</u> August 15 2006 health/nutrition 15 www.nytimes.com Jefferson-Madison Regional Library, Charlottesville, VA August 20 2006
Footnote 3: "Coffee News Roundup" <u>The British Coffee Association</u> www.britishcoffeeassociation.org February 3, 2005
Footnote 4: Lopez-Garcia, Esther Researcher at School of Medicine, Universidad Autonoma de Madrid, Spain <u>Times of India</u> April 25, 2006
Footnote 5: "Disease fighting – Colon Cancer" <u>The Coffee Science Organization</u> www.coffeescience.org January 24, 2005
Footnote 6: "Other Benefits of Coffee" <u>The Coffee Science Organization</u> www.coffeescience.org/fitness/diseasefight February 6, 2005
Footnote 7: Reduced risks referenced by Mitchell, Tedd, MD "Health Smart" <u>USA Weekend</u> "March 25-27, 2005 8, in <u>Consumer Reports</u> "Coffee vs. tea, Benefits and risks" November 2005 52 and by <u>The Coffee Science Organization</u> www.coffeescience.org January 24, 2005
Footnote 8: <u>Journal of the American Medical Association</u> June 9, 1999 and also referenced by <u>The British Coffee Association</u> www.britishcoffeeassociation.org February 3, 2005
Footnote 9: A Finnish study, a Dutch study, and one by the Harvard University School of Public Health are all referenced by "Disease Fighting" <u>The Coffee Science Organization</u> www.coffeescience.org January 24, 2005 References to reduced risks of Type II Diabetes can also be found in <u>USA Weekend</u> "Health Smart" March 25-27, 2005 8 and in <u>Consumer Reports</u> "Coffee vs. tea, Benefits and risks" November 2005 52
Footnote 10: Mitchell, Tedd, MD "Health Smart" <u>USA Weekend</u> March 25-27, 2005 8
Footnote 11: "Coffee vs. tea, Benefits and risks" <u>Consumer Reports</u> November 2005 52
Footnote 12: Mitchell, Tedd, MD "Health Smart" <u>USA Weekend</u> March 25-27, 2005 8
Footnote 13: "Antioxidant Powerhouse" <u>The Coffee Science Organization</u> www.coffeescience.org/fitness January 17, 2005
Footnote 14 Skatssoon, Judith "Coffee makes us say 'yes' "<u>Australian Broadcast Corporation</u> January 5, 2006 www.abc.net.au/science/news/stories/s1627382.htm March 7, 2007

Chapter 10 – The Future of the Coffee Drinking Species

Amy Musser, a recent James Madison University graduate ponders the future on the patio of one of Harrisonburg, Virginia's Daily Grind coffeehouses. (Photo by Nadia Mercer)

Field Guide Chapter 10 Highlights
- *A new breed at the coffeehouse*
- *Understanding coffeehouse evolution*
- *Future coffeehouse etiquette*
- *Predicting the future of your favorite drink*

A New Breed at the Coffeehouse

A photograph can be very revealing and this picture at the start of the chapter of a young lady musing about the future on the patio of a local Daily Grind franchise in Harrisonburg, Virginia tells us a lot about the changes that have already taking place regarding coffee and coffee habitats:

The location itself signifies that coffeehouses are no longer concentrated in the big cities of the Northeast or West Coast as was the case in 1960's and 1970's. They have spread to the small towns of America and are currently expanding at a rapid pace throughout the United States, Canada, Europe and the rest of the world.

The young lady herself, signifies the shift in coffee drinkers starting from the early European drinkers (male businessmen), through America's hippie culture in the 1960's, and the aging Baby Boomers of today many of whom grew up hanging out in old fashioned coffeehouses. As captured in this photograph. Most coffeehouse patrons are not only young, they are well educated, sophisticated, and the majority of the species is female.

Coffeehouses themselves have changed. They have become bright, open, and eye-appealing places to meet compared to many past versions. Like the picture depicts, many of them also have patios.

Perhaps the most disturbing aspect of the photograph to current coffee fanatics, is the fact that not only is her drink not a straight "cup of Joe" that many older Americans enjoy, it isn't even coffee. She is sipping a Mega Frozen Chai Latte! Blasphemy aside, this is certainly a harbinger of what the future holds. The new coffeehouse breed does not limit themselves to just coffee and coffee drinks; they are drinking tea, various iced drinks, smoothies, hot chocolates, steamers and everything in between.

Demographics Are Changing

This new breed of coffee drinker is not as countercultural, or rebellious as the old species, or necessarily plotting a revolution. The one strain of the species remaining (especially since the hippie days of the 1960's) is the artistic types. However these days whether authors, playwrights, poets, etc., they have business and marketing expertise. They use the coffeehouses for both creative and marketing purposes assisted of course by the internet. In this modern era, coffeehouses have become meeting places not only for students but for members of the business world, especially young professionals. But you will also see many retirees and young mothers with toddlers meeting at coffeehouses depending upon where you are. What's more, coffeehouses provide excellent coffee for a large variety of people who just stop by long enough to pick up their favorite drink on the way to work or for a quick coffee break.

Understanding Coffeehouse Evolution

Not only are coffeehouses on the rise in America and throughout the world, good coffee will continue to be their main product. The expansion of coffeehouses in America over the last twenty years has actually increased the percentage of young people drinking coffee. Now with the positive health benefits of coffee becoming well known and documented, even health conscious older ex-coffee drinkers who switched to tea are returning to their favorite drink. There will also be different drinks being offered mostly by large corporations who need to constantly develop new products in order to increase annual profits. But coffee is here to stay. Good quality coffee is even being served in major gas station chains as well as at fast food restaurants to satisfy consumer demand. And in addition to the normal gas, food, & lodging signs along our nation's highways, have you noticed those new ones with the familiar logo alerting you to the correct exit that has a Starbucks?

Coffeehouses of course align well with our high tech culture. Because of wireless technology, coffeehouses can now offer excellent high speed internet access to their patrons. More importantly, coffeehouses are becoming a place to meet, conduct business, and work on a project or school paper without feeling isolated. In fact a growing concern is that some patrons will cause coffeehouses to change their "stay as long as you like" policy, because they are actually using the space as their office for the cost of an espresso. Independent coffeehouse owners and coffeehouse chains alike are increasingly concerned about the Internet trends that facilitate the use of their establishment for all-day operations (see Prediction 6 in this chapter).

On the next page is this author's guide to coffeehouse etiquette for the future. If you plan to be spending considerable time in coffeehouses (and don't we all?), there is an emerging etiquette of behavior and consideration towards fellow patrons and the owner. As we move into the future with our portable PC's, Blackberry's, cell phones, iPods, slingboxes, and other devices, we need to follow guidelines similar to those below in order to protect our sacred sanctuary for years to come.

	RECOMMENDED COFFEEHOUSE ETIQUETTE
	(The Coffee Fanatic's keys to using coffeehouses for any length of time, for your virtual office, conducting business, etc.)
1.	Only occupy a single space. Don't take a table for four just to spread out your stuff.
2.	Don't buy the cheapest drink. If you don't like coffee drinks and prefer the Coffee of the Day, at least get a *Depth Charge* (shot of espresso) in it.
3.	Buy your coffee (for brewing at home), at the coffeehouse. Believe me, the owner knows if you are using his or her space all day and buying your "home" coffee at the supermarket.
4.	Occasionally buy a gift mug, new coffeemaker, grinder, etc. at the coffeehouse. Coffeehouses increasing carry an interesting array of quality products. If you are taking advantage of their space, you should at least buy from them.
5.	Do what you can to help the coffeehouse out – whether it is picking up some newspapers off the floor or vacating your spot to accommodate a larger group of customers.
6.	Tip the staff generously – and make sure that they know it.
7.	Be courteous to the other patrons and coffeehouse staff. Never talk on the cell phone inside the coffeehouse. Put your cell phone on "vibrate" & walk outside to answer all calls. Talk low when meeting with people, and never intrude on others' business or space.
8.	Occasionally, drop by the coffeehouse for lunch. Many of them serve sandwiches, wraps, or paninis. Again, this is just smart business, showing the coffeehouse that you are not just a one-drink loafer.
9.	Never nurse one drink all morning or all afternoon. About every 1 to 1&1/2 hours, buy yourself another drink.
10.	Do not use the coffeehouse for meetings of more than 2 people (unless you have permission, order lunch, etc.)

What Does the Future Hold for Coffee Drinkers?

A modern version of an old Irish expression states: *May you begin each morning with a smile on your face, a song in your heart, and a good cup of coffee in your hand!* The future certainly holds the promise of having a really good cup of coffee to start each day. Even if you are having that first cup at home as more and more major coffee companies are offering premium coffees and roasts. Plus average kitchen coffee makers will increase in efficiency and quality. Let's look at some future possibilities that could directly or indirectly affect us coffee fanatics - I call them,

"The Coffee Fanatic's Bold Predictions for the Future"

1: Enterprising Americans will grow and harvest the first North American coffee plants. Using hydro phonic growing techniques, the plants will be gowned indoors under perfect simulated conditions equal to the best mountainous regions of South and Central America.

2: One or all of the major food companies (Kraft, Nestle, etc. will start offering a full range of coffees, from their normal line to various estate grown gourmet coffees from around the World giving everyone across America more choices. And also eliminating the distinction between large coffee companies and specialty coffee roasters.

3: Better restaurants across America will offer customers a choice of single origin, coffees from the key growing regions of the world. Similar to a wine list, restaurants will show the estate where the coffee was grown, the date, and explain the flavor, acidity, aroma, and body of the coffees. You will be able to have your selection brewed to your liking.

4: It is inevitable, by 2010; a tall latte will cost $10. at Starbucks in most major cities of America!

5: Even newer medical evidence will come out in the next 5 years touting the health benefits of coffee. As a result, coffee drinks will overtake soft drinks as America's most popular non-alcoholic beverage.

6: By 2015, most Coffeehouses will need to establish maximum times per drink, monthly membership fees, or other forms of controlling their space as more and more consumers use them as office space and spend increasingly longer periods of time in them.

10: Convenience stores and gas stations will offer a coffeehouse-like range of coffeehouse espresso based drinks, from cappuccinos to lattes, using better coffees. (This has already begun at Sheets, a major gas station chain, as they now have a full-selection, espresso coffee bar installed at many of their locations.)

11: By 2012, increased demand for coffee from Asian countries (especially China) will create a shortage of coffee worldwide and prices will double from 2007 levels.

12: Coffeehouses will start offering more chocolate drinks to supplement their coffee drinks as well as hard chocolate as the public becomes more aware of the health benefits of chocolate which is rich in antioxidants.

13: Coffee will become the number one imported commodity of the United States, overtaking oil. This will come about due to both an increase in coffee consumption and a decrease in oil consumption because of alternative fuels.

14: Both the quality and quantity of coffee in certain South and Central American countries will suffer as more countries come under communist rule. This trend has already started in Brazil, Bolivia, Nicaragua and Venezuela as this book goes to print. These communistic regimes will ultimately meddle with the coffee industry in their countries and hinder the independent efforts of coffee farmers, processors and coffee growing cooperatives.

15: By 2012, technology and bio-technology will improve the decaffeination process. One possibility could come about through developing a new coffee plant that is caffeine free. Another possibility could involve brewing your favorite caffeinated coffee at home and then through the pressing of a button, your coffee maker will remove the caffeine. These processes will not affect the taste of the coffee like the current methods to remove caffeine do.

16: By 2015, more Americans will be drinking cold coffee drinks than hot coffee. Just look at the trend currently. Almost every coffeehouse is seeing their cold drink to hot drink ratio increase, even in the winter. Also check your local convenience store coolers. You will not only find Starbucks and the Nestlé company's cold coffee drinks, but also drinks that are hybrids of coffee and soft drinks (for example, Coca Cola's Blāk).

17: By 2015, there will be a plethora of coffee companies in America offering fresh, locally brewed coffee. This will come about as retiring Baby Boomers, who can't afford wineries, realize how relatively easy and inexpensive it is to become a Coffee Roaster.

18: In the future, there will be more Christian run coffeehouses in America and the clergy will start to see them as a natural extension of their church community and as a way to attract new members.

19: Asian countries will overtake South America to become the largest coffee producing region of the world.

20: Coffeehouses will become the most comfortable and safe, physical meeting place for people first communicating via the Internet. Additionally, innovative Web services will increase the use of the internet at coffeehouses, creating virtual communities of people who frequently visit them. These services will facilitate the ability of subscribers to interact with other customers regardless of whether they are actually in the coffeehouse.

Coffee Fanatic's Tip 31

<u>Here is a great energy tip for the future:</u>

Many of us take naps during the day recognizing the revitalizing benefit of a brief rest. In the future, have a cup of strong coffee first. Then, take your 10-15 minute nap. When you wake up the caffeine will just be starting to take affect, giving you a double "high-voltage" charge to face the rest the day.

The author's coffee bean bookends – Photo by Nadia Mercer

Section III – The Coffee Fanatic's Recommended Resources

Resources Highlights
- *Why a Secret List?*
- *The Best Kept Secret*
- *Websites*
- *Other Recommended Resources*

This Author's Secret List of Coffee Resources

While there are thousands of resources about the general subject of coffee, this list like the field guide itself is unique and reflects the presumed interest of the readers; the various types of Coffee Fanatics, who love coffee. It is unlike any other list ever complied. Just look in other books about the subject of Coffee. It is a combination of previously complied resources by the author, an admitted Coffee Fanatic, and those discovered while researching information for this book. The emphasis is on the Internet in that it has become an unparalleled resource in our society. And this is certainly true when it comes to information about coffee. The focus of the list is to categorize the pertinent information about coffee resources and to satisfy the vary levels of interest and thirst for information. While we know that this list will evolve over time, we trust this "secret" directory will save you time in getting to the information that you can use.

The Best Kept Secret – Your Local Coffeehouse

At the top of any list of resources about coffee should be an obvious one – but frankly, not that many people think of it. If you want to know more about a coffee drink, a coffee roast, a coffee maker, or for that matter anything associated with coffee; **ask the Owner or Barista at Your Local Coffee House.**

I can't emphasize how much I have learned from different coffeehouse owners through the years. After all this is their business and they are typically very willing to impart their knowledge and advice to you. Take advantage of this outstanding resource!

I. Coffee Websites

There is a plethora of information about the general subject of coffee on the Internet and it is your best resource after your local coffeehouse owner for doing further research or ordering hard-to-get supplies. Here are some of the best:

A. Coffee Blogs & Forums

http://www.bloggle.com - for the serious coffee fanatic

Author, Doug Cadmus

http://www.brewed-coffee.com/ - Covers a full range of topics from coffee history to coffee humor.

Author, Saloschin

http://www.javajeb.wordpress.com/ - Primary focus is on coffee roasting.

Author, unidentified

http://www.coffeeandcaffeine.com – A London-based Blog that is also a company that sells commercial espresso machines. They cover general coffee information as well as coffee health issues.

Author, CofCaf.co.uk

http://www.aboutcoffee.net/ - Called Badgett's e Journal, this online blog covers news about coffee from around the world.

Author, Badgett, Robert L.

http://www.coffeesage.com – Specializes in coffee & coffee product reviews

Author, Audrey, The Coffee Sage

http://www.perfectcoffees.blogspot.com – Focuses on news about coffee & the coffee industry, with recipes & trivia thrown in to the mix.

Author, Gresham, Gary

http://www.coffeeforums.com/ - a comprehensive forum moderated by coffee industry professionals covering a wide range of subjects.

B. Some Coffee Companies That Have Informative Websites

http://www.allegrocoffee.com/ - A very educational site that spans brewing tips to types of roasts to the coffee growing regions of the world.

http://www.bocajava.com/ - From terminology to recipes, a well designed & informative website

http://www.cafebritt.com/ - A Costa Rican Coffee company that offers everything from coffee to unique hand crafted gifts. (Also listed under **V.**, *Coffee Tours*)

http://www.dailygrindunwind.com/ - A large collection of coffee products from around the world.

http://www.gardfoods.com/coffee - Everything from the coffee plant to coffee & sex.

http://www.gloriajeans.com/ - From the history of coffee to coffee drink recipes.

http://www.illyusa.com/ - Everything espresso can be found at this website from one of the world's premier espresso roasting companies, including their famous collectable cups.

http://www.maxwellhouse.com – Includes products, coffee processing information, & recipes

http://www.peets.com/. - The famous coffee roaster has an excellent website with very informative information. The best glossary of flavor terms that I have come across.

http://www.realcoffee.co.uk/ - The Roast and Post Coffee Company offers unique coffees & coffee products from the U.K.

http://www.sangiorgiocoffee.com/ - Also, a coffee talk forum

http://www.starbucks.com/ - from Gingerbread lattes to the nutritional value of Starbucks' coffee drinks – it is all here.

http://www.thanksgivingcoffee.com/ - A fascinating and unique website that will inform you about both coffee and the various world-wide projects of a very socially responsible coffee company.

C. Coffee Equipment & Supplies

http://www.bodum.com/ - The very best in French Press coffeemakers, mugs, and other accessories.

http://www.campmor.com/ - A large camping and outdoor supplies company, they have a unique selection of coffee mugs and a few coffeemakers designed for camping, hiking and outdoor sports. However, their products, which include a small hand coffee grinder, are also excellent for coffee fanatics who travel frequently.

http://www.delonghi.com/ - The website of the world's foremost espresso machine manufacturer.

http://www.espressozone.com/ - Specializing in gourmet coffee, coffee brewers, & espresso accessories from around the world, Espresso Zone is a place to fill your various needs.

http://www.fantes.com/ - A total kitchen wares website, this is also an excellent source for all types of coffee equipment from espresso makers to coffee roasters to hard-to-find cappuccino & café au Lait cups.

http://www.sweetmarias.com/ - Everything from coffee brewers to espresso equipment to green beans for roasting, to educational material, this is an outstanding website to order hard-to-get supplies from

http://www.wholelattelove.com/ - A comprehensive and excellent on-line store that offers espresso machines & coffee makers from all the manufacturers. They offer one of the largest selections, competitive pricing and even an outlet store for refurbished models.

D. Coffee Houses

"Then I made the usual stop.
Coffee at the coffee shop"*

---

*<u>Same Old Saturday Night</u> S.Readon & S. Cohn – As originally sung by Frank Sinatra – recorded July 29, 1955 by Capitol Records

http://www.coffeehousenetwork.com/ - You can search this site by city to find coffeehouses. (Note: the site is in the process of being updated as this book goes to publication)

http://www.coffeehouse.com/ - Listing over 20,000 coffeehouses & shops in the USA, their coffeehouse directory is very comprehensive.

http://www.javawalk.com/index.html - Although dated, this website is excellent, listing some of the best coffeehouses in San Francisco. Read "Javaspot" for a real dose of coffeehouse culture.

GOING TRAVELING?

No need to miss a good cup of coffee!

Find the locations of your favorite coffeehouse chains in the city that you are traveling to. Most of them have a convenient look-up feature at their web site.

http://www.cariboucoffee.com/locations/index.asp -

http://www.dailygrindunwind.com/locations/

http://www.starbucks.com/retail/locator/default.aspx

http://coffeebean.com/location.aspx -

http://www.coffeebeanery.com/locations/default.asp

http://www.gloriajeans.com/storeLocator.aspx

http://www.seattlesbest.com/about/locations.aspx

http://www.spinelli-coffee.com/stores/index.asp - Tully's

http://www.portcityjava.com/LOCATIONS

PLUS: Don't forget the 540 Cracker Barrels for a really good, basic "Cup of Joe"- http://www.crackerbarrel.com

---

Note: Also see _Coffee Crazy: A Guide to the 100 Best Coffee Houses in America_ under **II, Recommended Books**)

E. Coffee Associations & Informational Organizations

http://www.ams.usda.gov/nop/ - Website of the United States Department of Agriculture's USDA Organic program

http://www.britishcoffeeassociation.org/ - The British are not just a country of tea drinkers and this informative website attests to their heavy drinking coffee habit.

http://www.coffeeresearch.org/ - For the serious coffee researcher

http://www.coffeescience.org/ - Also for the serious researcher, coffeescience.org is a service of the National coffee Association. The emphasis is on health related information.

http://www.coopcoffees.com/ - Website of Cooperative Coffees, a cooperative of US & Canadian coffee companies that focus on the import of Fair Trade & Organic coffees.

http://www.crsfairtrade.org/ - Website of Catholic Relief Services who have their own Fair Trade label plus a label for Nicaraguan coffee

http://www.ico.org/ - Website of The International Coffee Organization.

http://www.ncausa.org – Website of the National Coffee Association.

http://nationalzoo.si.edu/ConservationAndScience/MigratoryBirds/Coffee/Bird_Friendly/ - Learn all about Shade Grown and Bird Friendly coffees at this Smithsonian National Zoological website.

http://www.organicconsumers.org/ - Website of the Organic Consumers Association.

http://www.rainforest-alliance.org/ - Website of the Rainforest Alliance Organization

http://www.scaa.org/ - Website of the Specialty Coffee Association of America

http://www.transfairusa.org/ - Website of TransFair USA, the Fair Trade certifying organization.

F. Coffee – Newsletters/Zines

http://www.virtualcoffee.com/index.html - This on-line Quarterly coffee Zine, a division of Bellissimo, Inc, known as *Virtual Coffee* covers news about gourmet and specialty coffees. A well written & very professional newsletter.

http://www.ineedcoffee.com/ - This Monthly, a combination Zine & Blog furnishes a wide variety of information and news about coffee & coffee culture (take a look at the Caffeine Goddess).

http://www.coffeechatnews.com/cfml/signup.cfm - This is a monthly free electronic newsletter (sponsored by Dunkin Donuts) and written by Phil Lempert, who is also known as the Supermarket Guru. It covers various facts about coffee as well as new trends in the coffee industry.

http://www.coffee-explorer.com/ - A free electronic newsletter is offered covering new products, trends and world-wide news for both members of the coffee industry and for the general public.

http://www.thenewsflashcorporation.net/gloriajeans/ - The *Coffee Companion* is a free monthly electronic newsletter by Gloria Jean's. It is well written and covers everything from coffee humor to health issues regarding coffee.

G. Coffee – Ratings

http://www.coffeereview.com/ - This is the best, most professional rating service for reviewing coffees from around the world. It is run by coffee expert, Kenneth Davids. They use a 100-point system similar to the Wine Spectator.

http://www.rateitall.com/t-642-coffee - A consumer rating site comparing all the popular coffees from major companies as well as from smaller specialty companies. You will be surprised by some of these ratings.

http://www.coffeeratings.com/ - This site furnishes ratings on espressos served (and the coffeehouse atmosphere) at the approximate 400 coffeehouses in San Francisco.

H. Coffee – Miscellaneous

http://www.nationalgeographic.com/coffee/ - Like anything from National Geographic, this is a first class, professional site that will give you a world-wide perspective on coffee.

http://www.sallys-place.com/beverages - Covers food, beverages, & travel. Take the time to search for "coffee" & you will be rewarded with great information.

http://www.coffeeuniverse.com/ - Developed by Bellissimo Coffee InfoGroup, this is a comprehensive and well designed website covering every facet of coffee. It also has a form of a search engine to access both their data base and the Internet's about any aspect of coffee.

http://cocoajava.com/java_poster_shop.html - A great place to browse & purchase coffee-related posters

http://www.coffeegeek.com/guides - An interesting & informative website run by WebMotif Net Services, Inc. in

Vancouver, British Columbia. Espresso aficionados especially will enjoy this site.

http://www.koffeekorner.com/quotes.htm - A true Coffee Fanatic's type of website developed by Miku Sippy from Hong Kong. Although dated, this site will entertain and educate you with coffee history, health, trivia, and even coffee cartoons.

II Recommended Books about Coffee, Coffee Drinks & Coffeehouses

<u>*Coffee: A Cultural History From Around The World*</u> Milton, Ed S. (Astrolog Publishing House, Ltd., 2003)

<u>*Coffee: A Guide to Buying, Brewing, and Enjoying*</u> Davids, Kenneth (5th. Edition, St. Martin's Press, 2001)

<u>*Coffee: A Little Indulgence*</u> (G & R Publishing Company, 2005)

<u>*Coffee Basics*</u> Knox, Kevin & Sheldon Huffaker, Julie (John Wiley & Sons, Inc., 1997)

<u>*Coffee Crazy: A Guide to the100 Best Coffee Houses in America*</u> Bizjak, Marybeth (Aslan Publishing, 1996)

<u>*Espresso Served Here!*</u> Patricelli, Leslie & Gruening, Michelle (Gooddog Press, 1993)

<u>*Making Your Own Gourmet Coffee Drinks*</u> Tekulsky, Mathew (Crown Publishers, Inc., 1993)

<u>*The Coffee Book: Anatomy of an Industry*</u> Dicum, Gregory & Luttinger, Nina (The New Press, 1999)

<u>*The Joy of Coffee*</u> Kummer, Corby (Revised & Updated, Houghton Mifflin Company, 2003)

<u>*The Top 100 Coffee Recipes*</u> Ward, Mary (Wings Books, 1995)

The Totally Coffee Cookbook Seigel, Helene & Gillingham, Karen (Celestial Arts Publishing, 1995)

Uncommon Grounds Pendergrast, Mark (Basic Books, 1999)

III Coffee Magazines

Coffee & Cocoa International

Published Bi-Monthly   Subscription: (check publisher for US Price)

Coffee & Cocoa International, Office 8, Unit 1-2 Wyvern Estate, Beverley Way, New Malden KT3 4PH, UK. Tel: +44 (0) 20 8949 0088

Subscription: info@siemex.biz

An international magazine, published by Siemex International Ltd in the United Kingdom, reports on the growing, harvesting, processing, and selling of coffee and cocoa. While a trade magazine, it may be of interest if you want to keep abreast of trends and current coffee news from around the world.

Fresh Cup Magazine

Published Monthly   Subscription: $39. a year
(At time of publication)

Fresh Cup Magazine, P.O. Box 14827 • Portland, OR 97293-0827 • 503/236-2587

subscriptions@freshcup.com

Of primary interest to people in the coffeehouse business and other industry professionals, this magazine focuses on new trends and ideas in the retail coffee & tea business. Depending upon your degree of coffee fanaticism, the coffee drinker may also find it interesting.

IV Coffee Courses/Schools

Note 1: We purposely have not listed the various courses offered to people who either want to open a coffeehouse or become a barista since it is not a theme of this book. You can find out plenty of information about these subjects by searching the Internet. Below are courses of possible interest for true coffee fanatics who want to get a further appreciation of their favorite drink.

Pennsylvania College of Technology (part of Penn State)

Coffee 101   CON 556

Covers the history of coffee, types of coffees, and types of coffee drinks.

Register at 570-327-4775 or through their website; www.pct.edu.catlg/con556.shtml

Des Moines Area Community College

Coffee 101   CULA 702

An introductory course covering the world of coffee and the differences between brewing methods.

Register at 1-800-363-2127 or through their website; www.dmacc.edu/courses

Centre College, Danville Kentucky

The Cafés and Public Life

This course, by Professor Beau Weston focuses on coffeehouses and their social significance as well as an appreciation of coffee.

Register at 859-238-5714 or through their website; www.centre.edu/

McHenry County College, Illinois

Geography of Coffee

This course, by Professor Ted Erski, focuses on tasting different coffees and appreciating the differences in the different coffee growing regions of the world.

Register at 815-455-3700 or through their website; www.mchenry.edu/

Note 2: In addition to the learning resources listed above, check with your local colleges and schools for any courses that they may offer.

V Coffee Tours

The Cafe Britt Coffee Tour Mercedes Norte de Heredia, Costa Rica
1-800-462-7488 (1-800-GO BRITT)

Website: http://www.cafebritt.com/coffeetour/

A unique experience as Café Britt has been operating tours for over 15 years now and in fact, they offer a number of different tours depending upon your interests.

9:00 am, upon request and subject to availability plus 3:00 pm, daily from Dec. 15th to Apr. 30th Other times and dates offered for group reservations. Tours available with our without transportation. Tours vary in price so check their website for current pricing.

Holualoa Kona Coffee Company - Kona Le`a Plantation

77-6261 Mamalahoa Hwy, Holualoa Hawaii 96725
Toll Free: 800-334-0348

Website: http://www.konalea.com/index.htm

This is a free tour where you will learn what goes into one of the world's finest coffees from the tree to the cup. In addition to the estate's coffee orchards, guests can view the thriving mill and roasting operation that handles coffee for more than 100 nearby farms.

Monday to Friday 8 am to 4pm. Telephone 322-9937.

Selva Negra Mountain Resort and Coffee Estate
Km 140 Highway Matagalpa-Jinotega, Nicaragua
USA phone: 404-588-9171
http://www.selvanegra.com
A real bargain, once you get there, at $3.00 per person. This is a "shade-grown" coffee plantation plus Selva Negra is also a resort – check out the other activities available on their website.

Filadelfia Genuine Antigua Plantation

Antigua Guatemala

The R. Dalton Coffee Company has been growing coffee since 1870 in Guatemala and is a three time winner of the "Cup of Excellence" award. This tour will take you through every step of the coffee growing & harvesting operations.

There are two tours at 9 a.m. and 2 p.m. on Monday through Friday and one tour at 9 a.m. on Saturday.

Contact them at their Guatemala City Office:
R. Dalton Coffee Company
Tel: 011-502-2473-2601 through 9
Anillo Periferico 17-36
01011 Guatemala City
Zona 11
Guatemala, Central America

Website: http://www.rdaltoncoffee.com/5_0_tour.html

Index

A

Advertising
    Joe DiMaggio, **83**
    Juan Valdez, **24**
    Maxwell House solgan, **21**
Americano
    Description of, **43**
    Summary of, **45**
Arabica beans
    Columbian, **59**
    Marketed as gourmet coffee, **25**
    On labels, **68**
Arbuckle Brothers, **18**
Asian countries, **163**
Automatic Drip coffee maker
    Advantages of, **84**
    Description of, **82**

B

Baby Boomers, **158**, **164**
Badgett, Robert, **169**
Barista
    Mixing drinks like, **53**
Bellissimo Inc., **174**
Bins, coffee
    Buying coffee from, **69**
Bird Friendly, **114**
Bird Friendly Certification
    Overview of, **126**
Blackberry's, **160**
Blended coffee
    Motivation behind, **61**
    On labels, **68**
Blogs, coffee, **168**
Boca Java, **134**
Bodum, **170**
Books, about coffee, **176**
Brewing coffee
    For more than one person, **95**
    Trial and error approach, **95**
British Coffee Association, **173**
Buying coffee
    Recommendations, **66**, **67**

C

Cafe Au Lait
    Description of, **45**
    Summary of, **46**
Cafe Femenino, **134**
Cafe Mocha, **149**
Caffe Trieste, **24**
Caffeine, **149**
    Benifits of, **145**
Calories
    Breakdown by type of drink, **152**
    Changing type of drink, **154**
    Chart explaining, **153**
    In coffee drinks, **150**, **152**
    Tips on reducing in home drinks, **155**
Campmor, **170**
Cappuccino
    Cup for serving, **98**
    Description of, **43**
    Summary of, **45**
Caribou Coffee, **172**
Catholic Relief Services, **130**, **173**
Catholic Relief Services - Nicaragua, **115**
Central American countries, **163**
Chai Latte, **159**
Charitable causes
    Related to coffee, **133**
Coffee
    Medicinal purposes, **15**
    Quality of in early America, **19**

182 – The Coffee Fanatic's Guide

Coffee Bean, 172
Coffee Beanery, 172
Coffee brands
    Ariosa, 18
    Blue Anchor, 26
    Boca Java, 134
    Cafe Femenino, 134
    Eight O' Clock, 25
    Millstone, 26
Coffee break, 21
    Origin of, 24
Coffee certifications
    Range of, 115
Coffee Companies
    A & P Company, 18
    A & P, origin of, 20
    A& P, early brands, 22
    Chase & Sanborn, 18
    Chock full o' Nuts, 24
    Chock full o' Nuts, origin of, 21
    Folgers, orgin of, 20
    M.E. Swing Company, 21
    Maxwell House, 18
    Millstone, 26
    Nescafe, 22
    Peets Coffee & Tea, 25
    Proctor and Gamble, 26
    Seattle's Best, 60
    Starbucks, 60
Coffee Corps, 134
Coffee culture
    1990's to Present, 26
    American - key dates, 19
    American coffeehouses, 31
    Coffeehouse demographics, 34
    Current uses of coffeehouses, 160
    Emergence in America, 18
    Hippie Generation, 24
    Post World War II, 23
    Pre-World II, 22
Coffee drinks

Americano, 43
Basic types, 41
Cafe Au Lait, 45
Cappuccino, 43
Coffee of the Day, 45
Coffeehouse lingo, 50
Doppio, 43
Espresso, 43
Espresso as main ingredient, 40
Espresso con Pama, 43
Espresso Macchiato, 43
Espresso Romano, 43
How to order, 48
Latte, 44
Mocha, 44
Nomenclature, 39
Reference chart, 47
Sizes, 48
Typical coffeehouse menu, 42
Various combinations of, 48
Why coffeehouses make the best ones, 40
Coffee Fanatic
    Definition of, 3
    Determining type, 10
    Level of, 4
    Test, 4
Coffee farm workers
    wages of, 119
Coffee farms, 118
Coffee grinders
    In Early America, 20
Coffee growing countries
    Columbia, 59
    Countries producing some of the best coffee, 56
Coffee habits
    Cappuccino, 5
    Latte, 5
    Number of cups per day, 6
    Type of cup, 5

Index - 183

Coffee Kids, **135**
Coffee Makers
    How to select, **73**
    Key features of Automatic Drip makers, **85**
    Percolator, **22**
    Qualities of the older species, **74**
    Variety of, **72**
Coffee of the Day
    Description of, **45**
    Summary of, **46**
Coffee plants
    Arabica, **56**
    Description of, **56**
    Differences between, **58**
    Hybrid varieties, **118**
    Robusta, **56**
Coffee preferences
    Purchasing for the home, **6**
    Starting the day, **5**
    When traveling, **5**
Coffee prices
    At coffee shops, **31**
    Over time, **23**
Coffee producing countries
    By volume, **55**
Coffee quality
    Comparison of large chains, **108**
    Tips for finding, **106**
    When traveling, **105**
Coffee roasting
    Addition of chicory roots, **19**
    First commercial roaster, **20**
    Improvement - 19th. Century, **18**
    In early America, **16**
Coffee types
    100% Columbian, **58**
    Blended, **61**
    Columbian, **59**
    Flavored, **60**
    Gourmet, **60**
    Kona, **55**
    Specialty, **59**
Coffee-explorer.com, **174**
Coffeegeek.com, **175**
Coffeehouse culture
    Changes in future, **164**
    New Orleans, **15**
Coffeehouse evolution, **159**
Coffeehouse owners/managers
    Advice about calories, **151**
    Advice on blends, **62**
    Advice on coffee quality, **141**
    Best resource for information, **77**, **168**
    Concern for farmers & environment, **133**
    Developing new drinks, **40**
    Freshness questions, **90**
    Information on drinks, **152**
    Knowledge of organics, **125**
    Knowledge of various certifications, **129**
    Offering drink options, **46**
    Roast Recommendations, **96**
Coffeehouses
    American, **14**
    Culture and technology, **160**
    Description of a good one, **38**
    Design and location, **32**
    Franchises, **37**
    Geographical differences, **34**
    Green Dragon, **15**
    How to find a good one, **37**
    In America, Seventeenth Century, **15**
    In Berlin, **15**
    In England, **15**
    in Mecca, **14**
    In Paris, **15**

In Venice, **15**
Merchants in Philadephia, **15**
Profile of an Independent, **35**
Reasons people go, **30**
Tontine in New York City, **15**
Types of, **13**, **36**
Coffeeratings.com, **175**
Coffeereview.com, **175**
Coffeeuniverse.com, **175**
Cold water brewing process, **81**
Columbian coffee, **68**
Convenience store coffee, **108**
Coolatas, **151**
Cooperative Coffees label, **138**
Costa Rica, **119**
Courses, about coffee, **178**
Cowboy Coffee, **19**
Cracker Barrel
   Locations, **172**
   Quality Coffee, **108**
CRS Fair Trade Certification
   Overview of, **130**
Cup of Joe, **1**, **13**
   As a communication tool, **149**
Cups
   For serving coffee at home, **97**
   Measuring for brewing, **94**

D

Daily Grind, **172**
   Patio of, **158**
   Plantation Blend, **136**
   Project Hope Partnership, **136**
Dark roast - Definition of, **64**
Davids, Kenneth, **16**
Decaffeination
   Swiss Water Process, **25**
   Switch to 35 years ago, **143**
Delongi, **170**
Demographics
   Of coffeehouse customers, **159**
Desert pairings for coffee, **99**
Dunkin Donuts, **109**

E

Espresso
   Alternate way of making, **80**
   Description of, **43**
   Influence of, **16**
   Invention of machine, **16**
   Summary of, **45**
Espresso con Pama
   Description of, **43**
   Summary of, **45**
Espresso Macchiato
   Description of, **43**
   Summary of, **45**
Espresso Roast - Definition, **64**
Espressozone, **170**
Etiquette for coffeehouses, **160**
European immigrants, **21**

F

Fair Trade
   Lable of, **114**
   Purpose of, **118**
Fair Trade Certification
   Overview of, **121**
Fantes, **171**
Farming Cooperatives, **122**
Fast food chains, **108**
Flavored coffees, **60**
Flavors types of, **49**
Frappuccino, **151**
French Press
   Advantages and disadvantages, **75**
   For entertaining, **97**
French Roast - definition, **64**
Freshness of coffee beans chart, **65**
Fungicides
   Use of, **119**
Future predictions about coffee, **162**
Futures contracts, **117**

G

Garnishes
    Typical types, **49**
Gas station coffee, **106**
    Three questions to ask, **106**
Global Economy
    Coffee as part of, **117**
Gloria Jeans, **170**, **172**
Gourmet coffee, **60**
Grande hazelnut latte, **151**
Grande Latte, **149**
Green businesses
    A total Green business, **138**
    In the coffee industry, **116**
Greenhouse Effect
    Ways to reduce, **132**
Gresham, Gary, **169**
Grinders, coffee
    Types, **93**
Grinding coffee beans - tip, **93**
Grounds for Change Coffee, **138**

H

Health benefits
    Coffee vs. Green Tea, **149**
    Concerning Gallstones, **147**
    In connection with Cancer, **145**
    In connection with Heart
        Disease, **145**
Health benifits
    Associated with aging, **144**
    Coffee as source of
        antioxidants, **144**
    Various, **147**
Health issues
    Negative effects of coffee, **148**
    Past vs. present chart, **145**
    With coffee, **143**
Honduras, **117**
Hotel/Motel coffee
    Quality of, **111**

I

Insecticides, **119**
Instant Coffee, **22**
IPods, **160**
Italian Roast, **64**

J

Java, port of, **15**, **117**

K

Koffeekorner.com, **176**
Kosher certification, **116**

L

Labels - How to read, **67**
Latte, **26**
    1,843,200 versions of, **48**
    Cup for serving, **99**
    Description of, **44**
    Summary of, **45**
Light roast - definition of, **63**

M

MacDougall, Alice, **21**
Magazines, about coffee, **176**
Manual drip coffee maker, **74**
Mattera, Joseph, **96**, **100**
Maxium, **24**
McDonald's
    And Fair Trade coffee, **123**
Medical disclaimer, **143**
Medium roast - Definition of, **64**
Mexican coffee workers, **118**
Mexico, **125**
Migratory songbirds, **129**
Mocha
    Description of, **44**
    Summary of, **45**
Mocha, port of, **15**, **117**
Mr. Coffee, **72**

Myths about coffee, **148**

N

National Coffee Association, **143**
National Federation of Columbian
    Coffee Growers, **24**
National Geographic, **175**
Neapolitan flip coffee maker
    Advantages and
        disadvantages, **77**
    For brewing of espresso, **96**
New Orleans, **21**
Nicaragua Fair Trade, **130**

O

Organic coffee
    Certified USDA, **114**
    Discussion of, **126**
    Health benefits, **125**
    Overview of USDA
        certification, **124**
    Without formal certification,
        120
Other coffee spots
    When traveling, **104**

P

Packaging
    Arbuckles, **20**
    freshness valve, **25**, **69**
    In early America, **20**
    In vacuum-sealed tins, **20**
Parkinson's Disease, **146**
Peet, Alfred, **25**
Peets, **170**
Percolator coffee maker
    Advantages and
        disadvantages, **81**
Performance benefits
    Of coffee, **148**
Peru, **125**, **134**

Pod coffee maker, **86**
Pura Vida coffee, **135**
Purchase recommendations
    For use at home, **70**

Q

Quality
    As related to certifications, **120**
    ISO 9000 & ISO 14000
        standards, **137**

R

Rainforest
    Biodiversity of, **119**
    Discussion of eco-system, **127**
Rainforest Alliance, **114**, **115**
    Overview of, **128**
Reggio's, 21
Restaurant coffee
    What to look for, **111**
Roasting process
    Affects on aroma and taste, **64**
    Basic types, **62**
    Dates on packages, **69**
Roasts
    As indicated on packages, **68**
Robusta beans
    On labels, **68**
Roosevelt, Teddy, **21**

S

Schultz, Howard, **26**
Scientific Advisory Group, **144**
Seattles Best, **172**
Serving coffee at home
    Helpful hints, **102**
    Recommendations, **101**
    Time considerations, **101**
Seven-Eleven Stores, **109**
Shade Grown
    Overview of, **129**

Stamped on label, **114**
Sinatra, Frank, **171**
Single-origin coffee, **60**
  Compared to blended coffee, **68**
Slingboxes, **160**
Smithsonian Migratory Bird Center, **115**, **127**
Soot coffee, **54**
Specialty coffee
  Buying from coffeehouse, **60**
  On labels, **68**
Specialty Coffee Association of America, **59**, **174**
  Position on Fair Trade, **140**
Specialty coffee industry
  Success of coffeehouses, **60**
Specialty coffees
  Definition of, **59**
Starbucks, **172**
  Competing in commercial marketplace, **60**
  Early expansion, **26**
  Influence on culture, **17**
  Origin of, **25**
Stewart, Martha, **1**
Storing coffee beans, **66**, **90**
Stovetop Espresso coffee maker
  Advantages and disadvantages, **79**
Sustainable Agriculture Network, **114**, **128**
Sweet Marias, **171**

T

Thanksgiving Coffee, **136**, **170**
Tours
  Cafe Britt, **179**
  Filadelfia Gegunuine Antigua Plantation, **180**
  Holualoa Kona Coffee Company, **179**

Selva Negra Mountain Resort, **180**
Transfair USA, **115**, **174**
Travel tips, **112**
Tully's, **172**
Type II Diabetes, **147**

U

United States Department of Agriculture, **115**, **150**, **173**

V

Vacuum coffee maker
  Advantages and disadvantages, **78**
  For entertaining, **97**
Valdez, Juan, **24**, **58**
Vending machines, **24**
Vienna Roast - Definition, **64**
Vietnam War protests, **24**
Volume
  American purchases, **26**

W

Water
  Importance of in brewing a good cup, **91**
  Improving quality of, **92**
Websites, **168**
Whipped Cream
  Choices for coffee drinks, **49**
Wholelattelove, **171**

Y

Yemen, port of, **15**

Z

Zabars, **25**

Index to Tips

Did you miss some of our tips? We have thirty one of them throughout the book. Here is a quick index to all of them.

Coffee Fanatic's Tip 1: On buying Arabica beans	58
Coffee Fanatic's Tip 2: "Everyday" coffee	59
Coffee Fanatic's Tip 3: Buying Specialty coffee	61
Coffee Fanatic's Tip 4: On Buying blended coffee	62
Coffee Fanatic's Tip 5: Becoming aware of roasts	64
Coffee Fanatic's Tip 6: Buying, grinding and brewing	66
Coffee Fanatic's Tip 7: Check for roasted dates	69
Coffee Fanatic's Tip 8: Avoid Manual Drip maker	75
Coffee Fanatic's Tips 9 & 10: On the French Press	77
Coffee Fanatic's Tip 11: Using a Neapolitan Drip pot	78
Coffee Fanatic's Tip 12: On the stovetop espresso maker	80
Coffee Fanatic's Tip 13: Buying an Automatic Drip maker	85
Coffee Fanatic's Tip 14: Trying out a Pod maker first	86
Coffee Fanatic's Tip 15: Storing coffee beans	90
Coffee Fanatic's Tips 16 & 17: Types of water to use	92
Coffee Fanatic's Tips 18 & 19: About coffee grinders	93
Coffee Fanatic's Tip 20: Brewing for more than one	95
Coffee Fanatic's Tip 21, 22 & 23: Pairing recommendations	101
Coffee Fanatic's Tip 24: Questions to ask	106
Coffee Fanatic's Tip 25 & 26: Avoid while traveling	107
Coffee Fanatic's Tip 27: When dinning out	111
Coffee Fanatic's Tip 28: Bringing your own coffee	112
Coffee Fanatic's Tip 29: About medical studies	150
Coffee Fanatic's Tip 30: On reducing calories	155
Coffee Fanatic's Tip 31: "high-voltage" nap	165

Coffee Fanatics

We hope that you enjoyed this book

Now we would love to hear from you!

It's easy; send a quick e-mail to the author:

matt@coffeefanaticsguide.com

Send us an e-mail & you will be entered in our monthly drawing for a Coffee Fanatic's prize

We are interested in what you liked about the book and what you did not like, other comments, suggestions, etc.

In particular, we are interested in:

- ➤ Any other significant dates in American history and culture that are related to coffee (Chapter 1)
- ➤ Any additions to "Coffee House Lingo" (Chapter 3)
- ➤ Any coffee resources that are your favorites (Section III)
- ➤ And of course, any additional questions for our Coffee Fanatic's Test (Section I) will be greatly appreciated.

Note: You will soon be able to visit the Coffee Fanatic's website at **www.coffeefanaticsguide.com**. Under development with the first printing of this book, it will include useful information, tips, and tidbits about coffee when finished.

Fast Order Form

E-mail Orders: orders@coffeefanaticsguide.com
Fax Orders: 434-985-4264 (Send this form)
Telephone Orders: 1 800-362-1695 - Access Code: 25
(Have your credit card ready)
Mail Orders: Shenandoah Blue Ridge Media
Matt Peach
955 Carodon Drive
Ruckersville, VA 22968-3087

™

Please send the following number of *The Coffee Fanatic's Field Guide* book at $17.95 US each:

No._____

Sales Tax: Add 5% for books shipped to Virginia addresses

Shipping: United States - $4. for a single book. $2. for each additional book. **International:** $9. for a single book. $4.50. for each additional book.

Payment: MasterCard _____ or Visa _____

Acct. # (16 digits) _____

Expiration Date _____ **3 digit# from back** _____

Name on card: _____

Signature: _____

Note: A check is also an acceptable payment for mail orders.

- For information about ordering bulk quantities, contact **info@coffeefanaticsguide.com**